T0133587

Information Technology and Data in Healthcare

Using and Understanding Data

Information Technology and Data in Healthcare

Using and Understanding Data

David Hartzband

CRC Press
Taylor & Francis Group
Boca Raton   London   New York

CRC Press is an imprint of the
Taylor & Francis Group, an **informa** business

A PRODUCTIVITY PRESS BOOK

CRC Press
Taylor & Francis Group
6000 Broken Sound Parkway NW, Suite 300
Boca Raton, FL 33487-2742

International Standard Book Number-13: 978-0-367-18379-0 (hardback)

Library of Congress Cataloging-in-Publication Data

Library of Congress Control Number:2019948478

Visit the Taylor & Francis website at
http://www.taylorandfrancis.com

and the CRC Press website at
http://www.crcpress.com

To Maureen

Publisher's Note

David J. Hartzband passed away in April 2019 shortly after finishing the manuscript for this book. I had the honor and privilege of meeting David on several occasions. I found him to be a thoughtful, caring, and incredibly smart individual who had a passion for information technology in healthcare. He will be missed by his family, friends, and colleagues. Health Information Technology has truly lost a champion.

Kristine Rynne Mednansky
Senior Editor
Taylor & Francis Group, LLC
CRC Press, HIMSS Publishing

Contents

Contents

Preface

Not everything that can be counted counts, and not everything that counts can be counted.

—Often attributed to Albert Einstein, but actually by William Bruce Cameron*

You can bail water 24/7, and no matter how good you are at not sinking, you still have a hole in your boat.

—Kelli Jae Baeli, Crossing Paths†

The fact of the matter is that there are several holes in the healthcare boat. They include access, coverage, disparities in care, reimbursement, use of both clinical and information technology – I could go on ... and the boat **is** sinking, despite all the bailing that we are doing. One of the biggest issues, and one of the biggest opportunities, is information technology. Healthcare information technology (HIT) can be addressed and improved without having to do major surgery to the healthcare system in general. It will, however, require large changes in both the technology used and how it is used. That will mean organizational and cultural changes that will be difficult (purposely understated).

---

* William Bruce Camerson, 1963, *Informal Sociology, a Casual Introduction to Sociological Thinking*. New York: Random House, p. 13.
† Kelli Jae Baeli, 2005, *Crossing Paths*. Oklahoma, OK: Indie Literati Press.

This book is about realizing the potential in the use of information technology in healthcare. The core of this potential is healthcare data – what it is, how to manage and use it, how to make decisions based on it, and how the hardware and software infrastructure used by healthcare organizations needs to change to optimize the use of data in order to meet the needs of healthcare providers and patients.

Audience – This book is aimed at decision-makers in healthcare organizations. These include the C-suite, that is CEO, COO, CFO, CMO, CIO, etc., as well as the people in charge of information technology (applications and infrastructure), clinical decision-making, analytics, and any other staff who make, or assist in making, decisions. It is also aimed at policy analysts who evaluate HIT strategy and practice, and at legislators and regulatory officials who are responsible for directing and guiding government policy on healthcare and HIT.

Importance – It is hard to overestimate the importance of understanding data in the current and near-future healthcare environment. Many healthcare organizations today have hundreds of gigabytes (GBs, 10^9 bytes) of data, and the largest ones have hundreds of terabytes (TBs, 10^{12} bytes) to tens of petabytes (PBs, 10^{15} bytes). This includes data on the demographics, insurance coverage, and clinical status of individual patients, as well as population and public health data, the organization's financial data, and many other types of strategic data without which the organization could not function. The collection management and use of this data are becoming more and more important as healthcare evolves to a more value-based reimbursement model. Understanding exactly what data is, what its uses and limitations are, and how the healthcare data landscape is evolving will be essential for healthcare organizations to continue to function. These topics are the focus of this book.

Comparison – Amazon lists 1,032 books on healthcare data as available for purchase (10 July 2017). The vast majority of these are "how-to" books, that is:

- How to provide privacy and security for healthcare data
- How to analyze large amounts of healthcare data
- How to analyze small amounts of healthcare data
- How to analyze healthcare data for quality and performance improvements
- How to recognize if you are analyzing healthcare data
- etc.

The list is almost endless. What appears to be lacking is the bigger picture with respect to data. How are we to think about data? What's important about it? What can data analysis tell us? Can we develop a deeper awareness of data that allows us to use it in more productive ways?

Answering these questions requires addressing what data is and how it can be used with more than a "how to" approach. Examining what we can believe about data, how we know what we know about data, and what the implications of this examination are for data analysis in the largest sense are the core of this book.

This book is deeply technical in terms of data and the infrastructure needed to deal with the acquisition, management, and utilization of data in healthcare. It does not give prescriptions for business strategy or IT product development, but it does make recommendations for developing the awareness and culture necessary to productively use data in order to improve clinical and operational outcomes in healthcare.

Description and Chapter Outlines

The book is structured in eight chapters and a summary. The plan for the book is to start by examining data: what it is, what we can know about it, how it is structured, where it fits in, and how we use it to make meaning and understand the world around us. It then progresses to ask many of the same questions about analysis and to apply the understanding of these topics to an examination of data analysis, especially data analysis in healthcare. The book then describes both the current information technology environment in health information technology and how this environment, infrastructure, and application need to evolve in order to deal with the different types and increased volume of healthcare data that will be important in the near future (present to 5 years). The book puts data and data analysis into the context of improving clinical and operational outcomes in healthcare, including current and near-future developments in applying machine intelligence and machine learning to healthcare data. Finally, it describes the necessary evolution of data and the use of data in healthcare.

The chapters include anecdotes and examples so that the points made are illustrated by the author's experience. The Contents gives an outline of the chapters and their subtopics.

About the Author

David Hartzband was the director of Technology Research at the RCHN Community Health Foundation, New York. In his role at the foundation, he spearheaded the organization's continued evaluation, assessment, and findings relating to health information technology. Recent projects included the deployment of a contemporary (Hadoop-based) analytic stack into community health centers, and working with the executive and operations staff to understand and use this resource; the design and execution of population health projects at community health centers and primary care associations; the redesign and deployment of an updated health information technology infrastructure for a large primary care association; and the assessment of data quality in electronic health records of healthcare practices.

He brought more than two decades of diverse experience in the private and public sectors as a consultant, executive, and technology industry leader. He was founder and principal of PostTechnical Research, a trend analysis and technology strategy consulting firm. Previously, he was technology vice president of the Collaboration in the Content Management Software Group of the EMC Corporation. He also served as the chief technology officer for several technology companies, including Documentum, eRoom Technology, Agile Software, Upstream Consulting, and Riverton Software.

He was a consulting software engineer and senior technologist at the Digital Equipment Corporation from 1983 to 1995, where he held a variety of positions, including architect for Digital's relational database system (Rdb) at V1 and V2, architect for ObjectBroker, a distributed, object-based development and execution environment, technical director for manufacturing software, and chief scientist for the Artificial Intelligence Technology Group.

He authored numerous technical reports and journal articles in mathematics, artificial intelligence, concurrent engineering, and cultural anthropology. He served as an adjunct faculty member at both Stanford University (Computer Science Department and Knowledge Systems Laboratory), California, and the Massachusetts Institute of Technology (Leaders for Manufacturing Program). He was most recently a research scholar at the Institute for Data Systems and Society at the Massachusetts Institute of Technology.

Chapter 1

Introduction – Data Is Essential

Making the statement "data is essential" seems premature given that we could argue that we don't know specifically what data is* yet. The next chapter will cover what data is in detail, so let's agree to defer specific definition(s) until then and use data in the sense of factual information. So why is data essential in healthcare. Most of the work I've done in healthcare has focused on the use of factual information about an individual's health status, or the use of factual information about a group or population's health status in order to improve treatment and clinical outcomes for the individual or population. Healthcare policy currently has defined a set of goals embodied in the Triple (or Quadruple) Aim.† These goals include enhancing patient experience, improving population

---

* While *data* is clearly the plural of the noun *datum*, it also has a standard use as an abstract, mass noun (like *information*) for which it takes a singular verb and modifiers (*Merriam-Webster*, https://www.merriam-webster.com/dictionary/data). This is the form that the word data is used in this book.
† T. Bodenheimer and C. Sinsky, 2014, From Triple to Quadruple Aim: Care of the Patient Requires Care of the Provider. *Annals of Family Medicine,* November, 12(6): 573–576. doi:10.1370/afm.1713

health, reducing costs, and improving the work life of health-care providers.

It is clear that data plays an important role in each of these goals:

- Enhancing patient experience
  - There are two major aspects to enhancing the patient's experience: first is improving the healthcare outcome for the patient and second is improving how the patient and their family, caregivers, etc., experience the interaction with the healthcare establishment (doctors, other providers, hospitals, health centers, other treatment facilities, etc.). Improving outcomes requires access to and analysis of the patient's clinical data in order to do diagnosis, treatment planning, care coordination, and all the other things that constitute care.

    Improving the patient's and their family's and caregiver's experiences requires the communication of data so that all parties have the information they need to interact with the healthcare professionals providing care and to make the necessary decisions. This communication facilitates the trust that's needed in order for the entire healthcare experience to be improved for all parties.
- Improving population health
  - Addressing population health requires:
    - Identifying specific populations
    - Stratifying the individuals in the population with respect to the prevalent healthcare risks
    - Planning and executing interventions to reduce those risks and improve individual outcomes
      This is not possible without access to comprehensive data about the population(s) and the analysis of this data in order to identify and stratify risks.
- Reducing costs
  - Clinical and financial data need to be analyzed together in order to determine the cost of care (per capita and

along other dimensions such as per provider, per location, etc.). These results can then be used to plan cost reduction measures as well as compare costs over time in order to define the trend in costs.

▪ Improving the work life of providers
  – Data is also important in determining work and life conditions for providers and then in planning changes and/or interventions to improve the quality of their work life.

Today most healthcare organizations have 1–5 terabytes (1 TB = 10^{12} or, more formally, 2^{40} bytes) of data. This does not include image or device data. How much data is this? By comparison, the printed material in the Library of Congress is about 8–10 TBs. Of course, small organizations, such as community health centers and rural hospitals, have less data, in the 2–3 TB range, while large organizations, such as large urban hospitals (Mass General, Boston, Massachusetts, or Cedars Sinai, Los Angeles, California) may have much more – up to 1–5 petabytes (1 PB = 10^{15} or, more formally, 2^{50} bytes, a lot of data). Some very large healthcare organizations, such as Kaiser Permanente, have 10s of petabytes of data. This data includes individual patient clinical (electronic health record, EHR); demographic and logistic (scheduling, etc.) information; patient financial claims and payments; social determinants; cost accounting; inventory and ordering; registry; and operational types of information. Increasingly, it will also include clinical data from heterogeneous sources such as partner organizations, various types of independent provider associations, health information exchanges, and accountable care organizations. Additional sources will include population and public health data from public and private sources, macro- and microeconomic data from state and federal sources, and other data that we don't anticipate yet. The consensus is that this data will increase at 40%–60% a year – that is, it will double every 2 years! This means that most organizations will have

20 TBs of data in 6 years and the largest organizations may have in the range of 15–20 PBs in this timeframe. The technical implications of this growth in the amount of data to be managed and used will be addressed in Chapter 5.

It's fall, 2018. According to the Centers for Disease Control (CDC), 86.9% of office-based physicians were using an EHR system as of (1st quarter) Q1 2017.* This means that the vast majority of providers† are generating electronic data as part of their clinical practice. How did we get here? Providers, for the most part, did not decide to convert their practices to electronic records spontaneously, although some healthcare practices did just this as early as the 1960s. The Mayo Clinic adopted an EHR system sometime around 1963 and Eclipsis (now part of Allscripts) was developed in 1971 for the El Camino Hospital (Mountain View, California) by the Lockheed Corporation.‡ Most providers and healthcare organizations, however, adopted EHR systems (and other network-based record systems) because of federal regulations. These include the Health Information Technology for Economic and Clinical Health Act (HITECH), which is Title XIII of the American Recovery and Reinvestment Act (2/2009, Pub.L. 111-5, ARRA) and the Patient Protection and Affordable Care Act (3/2010, Pub.L. 111-148, ACA), as well as changes to the Center for Medicare and Medicaid Services (CMS) Physicians Fee Schedule (PFS 2012–2016) and the Medicare Access and CHIP Reauthorization Act of 2015 (MACRA, 4/2014, Pub.L. 114-10). In particular, the HITECH Act established guidelines for increased Medicare and Medicaid reimbursement if specific criteria were met for the use of electronic health records. These criteria

---

* https://www.cdc.gov/nchs/fastats/electronic-medical-records.htm

† Healthcare provider is defined as: a doctor of medicine or osteopathy, podiatrist, dentist, chiropractor, clinical psychologist, optometrist, nurse practitioner, nurse-midwife, or clinical social worker, who are authorized to practice by the state and performing within the scope of their practice.

‡ https://www.beckershospitalreview.com/healthcare-information-technology/a-history-of-ehrs-10-things-to-know.html

were called Meaningful Use (MU) requirements and there were three stages, starting with Stage 1 in 2009, Stage 2 in 2011, and Stage 3 in 2017.* In 2015, MACRA re-established the requirements for enhanced reimbursement to include a Value-Based Payment Modifier (VBPM), Physician Quality Improvement Program (PQRS), and Merit-Based Incentive Payment System (MIPS), and it continued the Meaningful Use (MU) program at Stage 3. One thing worth noting about the MIPS program is that it requires healthcare organizations to begin working to improve the health of populations as well as individuals. This requires both additional data and new types of analysis in order to identify populations that are at risk for various health outcomes and to be able to plan clinical and other types of interventions to address population-level issues.

This set of legislation and regulations ensures that healthcare organizations and individual providers continue to use EHR systems that are certified by the Office of the National Coordinator, Department of Health and Human Services (HHS).† This, in turn, ensures that the clinical, demographic, and other data captured by EHRs continues to grow at ever increasing rates as described above, and that processes for the capture, management, and use of this data become more and more important over time. It is worth noting that this entire regulatory body of material is currently under revision and that the HHS appears to be going through a phase of minimizing regulation. It is not clear what the regulatory landscape will look like in 3–5 years or what requirements for data capture and use healthcare organizations will need to meet.

One thing is clear regardless of this future direction – the requirement to use electronic health records has changed the way we think about and use data in healthcare.

---

* https://www.cdc.gov/ehrmeaningfuluse/timeline.html
† https://www.cms.gov/Regulations-and-Guidance/Legislation/ EHRIncentivePrograms/Certification.html

Chapter 2

What Is Data?

This is a book about data, but in order to understand and use data, or even to write about it, we need to have a common understanding of what it is. The following are several definitions of "data":

- Factual information (such as measurements or statistics) used as a basis for reasoning, discussion, or calculation
- Information in digital form that can be transmitted or processed
- Information output by a sensing device or organ that includes both useful and irrelevant or redundant information and must be processed to be meaningful*
- A set of values of qualitative or quantitative variables†

What do these definitions tell us? Data is a term for facts derived from measurement or analysis that can be useful, irrelevant, or redundant, and that generally must be processed in some way to be interpretable. This is interesting, but it does raise other questions; for instance, if data is factual information, then what are facts? A common definition is as follows:

---

* https://www.merriam-webster.com/dictionary/data
† https://en.wikipedia.org/wiki/Data

> A fact is a statement that is consistent with reality or can be proven with evidence. The usual test for a statement of fact is verifiability – that is, whether it can be demonstrated to correspond to experience. Standard reference works are often used to check facts. Scientific facts are verified by repeatable careful observation or measurement (by experiments or other means).*

So, facts can be proven and/or verified. This means that they are one of the following: true, false, or untested, and this has implications later on. Actually, there are circumstances when facts can have more than one of these statuses, but this is in reference to models and model theory, which is about what facts mean. This is not relevant for us here.† We are concerned here with what we can know about facts, as this will tell us what we can know about data.

Some years ago (no – longer ago than that …), I was lecturing at the Knowledge Systems Laboratory at Stanford University, California. We were working on expert or rule-based systems (see Chapter 7) to address a variety of problems including medical diagnosis. At the time, we tended to talk about a hierarchy of types of knowing that included data, information, knowledge, and wisdom. We had an inchoate understanding that each of these "levels" was in some sense more general or somehow deeper than the levels below it, but actual definitions tended to be ambiguous. A substantial amount has been written on this hierarchy in the last 40 years,‡ but I think the most coherent view of this has been

---

* https://en.wikipedia.org/wiki/Fact
† D.J. Hartzband, 2015, Model Brokerage: Concepts and a Proposal. Engineering Systems Division Working Paper. ESD-2015-08. doi: 10.13140/RG.2.1.4829.2967. Massachusetts Institute of Technology, Cambridge, MA.
‡ https://en.wikipedia.org/wiki/DIKW_pyramid

developed by Gene Bellinger (and his colleagues). Bellinger*
has given the following definitions:

- Data – Unorganized facts
- Information – Data organized with respect to the understanding of relations
- Knowledge – Information organized with respect to the
  understanding of patterns
- Wisdom – Knowledge organized with respect to the
  understanding of principles

This is still quite general, but it does give us a better idea of
the ways in which the elements at each level can be used.

In our sense, data, and especially healthcare data, is
interpreted by its organization with respect to the relations
between its different elements (often by storage in a relational
database or another type of data store). It can also be (statistically) analyzed in order to refine and/or discover additional
relations, and they can be more deeply analyzed (model building and discovery) to elicit patterns. Much of the rest of this
book will address this interpretation.

Data and Epistemology

In order to look at what we can know about data, we have to
talk about epistemology. Epistemology is the study of the theory of knowledge; it has been a focus of inquiry since at least
the 5th century BCE starting with Anaxagoras and continuing
with the 4th century BCE Greek philosophers Socrates, and
especially, Plato and Aristotle. The concepts of these think-
ers have shaped our idea of what can be known and how it

---

* G. Bellinger, D. Castro, and A. Mills, 2004, Data, Information, Knowledge, and
  Wisdom. Available at: www.systems-thinking.org/dikw/dikw.htm, accessed:
  February 5, 2006.

can be known, but they are not particularly relevant for our inquiry about data.*

In the 23 or so centuries since Aristotle, a huge body of work has been done on what we can know and how we know it. Contemporary epistemology appears to have passed through a number of phases and has arrived today at a very fragmented and confused state (in my opinion). Perhaps the most relevant modern (but not current) development is the work of the Vienna Circle in the 1920s and 1930s in defining an epistemology of "logical positivism."[†] This view is characterized by the principle that statements are cognitively meaningful only to the extent that they are empirically verifiable, and that the knowledge claims of systems such as logic and mathematics are justified only on formal grounds, that is through the status of their axioms and premises. The group was strongly influenced by Wittgenstein's concept "the meaning of [a] sentence is its verification."[‡] In fact, one of the leaders of the Circle, Moritz Schlick, met with Wittgenstein in 1930 to discuss this very proposition. This set of views held by the Circle could be reduced to Rudolph Carnap's principle that empirically significant statements must be such that experiential support for them or for their negation is at least conceivable.[§]

---

* https://www.britannica.com/topic/epistemology/
  The-history-of-epistemology#ref59970
† T. Uebel, 2016, Vienna Circle. *The Stanford Encyclopedia of Philosophy* (Spring 2016 edition), E.N. Zalta (ed.). https://plato.stanford.edu/archives/spr2016/entries/vienna-circle/
‡ L. Wittgenstein, 1921, Logisch-Philosophische Abhandlung. *Annalen der Nat. u. K. Philosophie* 14, pp. 185–262. Translated by C. Ogden, 1922, *Tractatus Logico-Philosophicus*, London. Revised edition 1933. Reprinted 1983, London: Routledge & Kegan Paul.
§ R. Carnap, 1928, *Scheinprobleme in der Philosophie (Pseudoproblems in Philosophy)*. Berlin, Germany: Bernary. In R. Carnap, 1928, *Der logische Aufbau der Welt*, Berlin, Germany: Bernary. Translated as *The Logical Structure of the World*, Berkeley, CA: University of California Press, 1967, pp. 301–343. R. Carnap, 1930, Die alte und die neue Logik. *Erkenntnis*, 1: 12–26. Translated as The Old and the New Logic, in A.J. Ayer, 1959, *Logical Positivism*. New York: The Free Press, pp. 60–81.

More recently, epistemology appears to have fragmented into a large number of different approaches and schools of thought. These include (but aren't limited to): historicism, empiricism, idealism, rationalism, constructivism, pragmatism, naturalism, skepticism, contextualism, internalism (simple and access-based), ethicism, and personal epistemology.* This list spans the range from the strictest formalism to the idea that truth is based on the context and/or the ethics of a statement, and finally to the concept that individuals develop their own views about knowledge and knowing in order to make meaning. Most recently arguments about justification and belief seem to be the prevailing focus for philosophers of knowledge. Two of these "isms" deserve a bit more description.

Moral epistemology[†] – Some recent work in epistemology has emphasized that moral value(s) of facts are to be considered in the examination of knowledge just as much as measured and/or inferred facts.[‡] This inevitably includes a good deal of discussion about the justification of belief, the density and complexity of these concepts being part of the criticism of this approach. This is very far from the verifiability criteria of the logical positivists and, of course, Wittgenstein may have had the last word on this when he wrote referring to ethics as his last thesis in the *Tractatus Logico-Philosophicus*, "Wovon man nicht sprechen kann, darüber muss man schweigen."[§]

Contextualism[¶] – Contextualism is the principle that the truth of an assertion can vary with the context in which that assertion is made and/or evaluated. Consider the following statement that your doctor might make to you.

---

[*] J. Pryor, 2001, Highlights of Recent Epistemology. *British Journal for the Philosophy of Science*, 52: 95–124.

[†] https://plato.stanford.edu/entries/moral-epistemology/

[‡] Cf. W. Rottschaefer, 1998, *The Biology and Psychology of Moral Agency*, Cambridge: Cambridge University Press. Or R. Campbell and V. Kumar, 2012, Moral Reasoning on the Ground, *Ethics*, 122: 273–312.

[§] L. Wittgenstein, 1921, Logisch-Philosophische Abhandlung, op. cit. "Of that which we cannot speak, We must pass over in silence."

[¶] J. Pryor, 2001, Highlights of Recent Epistemology. *British Journal for the Philosophy of Science*, 52: 95–124.

She says, "Your blood pressure has been high lately." Provided that we can agree on how to evaluate what high means with respect to blood pressure, we then realize that the truth of this statement may vary depending on what recent data range is selected for evaluation, as your blood pressure may have been higher during a specific recent period but is now normal. Much of the current effort in this area is focused on the theory of "relevant alternative theories" and whether a priori justification (in belief) is possible. The idea of relevant alternatives concerns whether we need to have evidence to disprove an alternative theory in order to be able to believe in the base theory. Pryor's (op. cit.) example for this is the assertion that a specific animal is a zebra and the relevant alternative theory that the specific animal is a donkey painted to look like a zebra. Do we have to have evidence that the animal is not a painted donkey in order to actually believe that it is a zebra. There is some disagreement among epistemologists as to whether this is the case or not. Contextualism can be thought of an extended form of logical positivism in that it requires evidence to determine the truth of an assertion; it also asserts that the same statement may have different truth values depending on the context it is made or evaluated in.

OK – so there is such a thing as the study of the theory of knowledge. Does this have any meaning for our ideas about data and healthcare data in particular? The real question is "Does understanding how knowledge gets its meaning help us to understand data and particularly healthcare data in any particular way?" The first thing we need is to have is a definition of knowledge that we can agree on. The *Merriam-Webster* dictionary defines knowledge in several ways, of which the most relevant appears to be: "the fact or condition of knowing something with familiarity gained through experience or association."* According to this definition, knowledge itself

---

* https://www.merriam-webster.com/dictionary/knowledge

is a fact and should be subject to verification, or, as Carnap stated (see earlier), experiential support for this knowledge or its negation must at least be conceivable. This tells us that, according to this major thread of epistemology, knowledge is a set of facts such that the facts making up the knowledge and the facts making up its constituents must be verifiable empirically, or at least their verification must be conceivable. A stronger form of this statement is that their verification must, at least, be feasible. This is the form in which we'll understand and interpret knowledge. We can now address our definition and understanding of healthcare data.

What Is Healthcare Data?

In the example of contextualism above we used blood pressure as an example of data, but what do we actually mean by data in healthcare? Earlier in this chapter I stated that "data is factual information derived from measurement or analysis," and that "facts are statements consistent with reality or that can be proven with evidence" – that is they are verifiable.

Healthcare data, therefore, means facts derived in a healthcare context by measurement or analysis and that are verifiable in that context. When your healthcare provider reports that your blood pressure is 145/75, your body mass index (BMI) is 22.4 and your average blood glucose level (HbA1c) is 6.8; these are facts whose values were measured (or derived from measurement as in the case of BMI) at a specific time and place, and that could be measured again at another time and place. At that subsequent time, your provider might reasonably expect the second set of measured facts to be relatively similar to the previous set. Deviations might be an indication of some change in your health status. This is true of most of our personal healthcare information (PHI). It is facts that are either directly measured or derived from these direct measurements.

What about other types of healthcare data? If we say that 38% of the patient population at a specific hospital has Type 2 diabetes, we are making several types of statements about facts and analysis. First, we are stating that we have a definition for Type 2 diabetes based on fact. We diagnose (adult) patients with Type 2 diabetes as follows:

- Fasting plasma glucose (FPG) ≥ 126 mmol/dl (7 mmol/l)
- Random plasma glucose (RPG) ≥ 200 mmol/dl
- Two-hour post-load glucose ≥ 200 mmol/dl
- HbA1c level ≥ 6.5 on two serial tests (3–5 months apart)

Second, we are stating that we have these measurements for a large and known percentage of the patient population. Both of these diagnostic criteria are measurements or sets of measurements. Third, we can analyze the patient population for the diabetes criteria and derive a percentage of the population that exhibits Type 2 diabetes – 38% in this case. All of this was done with measured facts or facts derived from analysis, that is … data.

So, what can we say now about data? We have a definition, or at least an understanding of what it is in general. We have some background about how to think of it in relation to what we can know and how we know it, and we understand what healthcare data is, in general, made up of.

- Data is a set of facts generated from direct or derived measurement or analysis that can be useful, irrelevant, or redundant, and that generally must be processed in some way to be interpretable.
- Facts are statements about the world. We establish the veracity of these facts through the process of verification. Verification can be through the comparison of:
  - Independent but identical facts (values such as blood pressure or random plasma glucose) measured at the same time

- Independent but identical facts (values such as blood pressure or random plasma glucose) measured at different times
- Measured facts with large-scale, verified measurements in separate data stores or collections, such as the percentage of people that have hypertension at a specific clinic versus the same percentage in the Centers for Disease Control (CDC) QuickStats database (national figures)
- Other means of comparison such as comparison with values in predictive models, etc.

For all the many thousands of pages written discussing the concepts of belief, justification, contextual variability, or the personal meaning of facts (that is epistemology or the study of the theory of knowledge), we still know facts directly from their statement and, at least in science and medicine, we base our belief in these facts on our ability to verify them. This is the very essence (at least as I understand and practice it) of science. We establish facts either by direct measurement or by the analysis of direct measurements. We don't establish facts by deep introspection or by the exploration of pure concepts. If we need to know someone's blood pressure or fasting plasma glucose, we measure it. If we need to know the percentage of Type 2 diabetics in a specific population, we aggregate measurements from individuals and analyze them – that is, we produce a derived fact. We might perform meta-analysis or simulation in order to explore a general statement (hypothesis), but, at some point, we need to have facts that can be verified to establish the truth or credibility of the statement.

A Short Note on Amounts of Data

The topic of "big data" will be discussed in Chapter 5, on data analysis, but a short discussion on amounts of data is appropriate here. Some time ago (April 2011), John Halamka, the CIO of Beth Israel Deaconess Medical Center (BIDMC) in Boston, Massachusetts, estimated that BIDMC had 250,000 patients and generated about 80 MB of structured data a year for each patient. This is primarily data in the center's EHR system and does not include audio, images, and video that may also be stored as clinical data.* More recently other estimates have doubled this amount to around 150 MB per patient per year for "average" patients and 350–500 MB per year for complex patients.

---

* J. Halamka, April 6, 2011, The Cost of Storing Patient Records. http://geekdoctor. blogspot.com/2011/04/cost-of-storing-patient-records.html

Chapter 3

Data and Culture

Data Appreciation and Awareness

Appreciation – The act of recognizing or understanding that something is valuable or important (*Cambridge English Dictionary*)

So we have data, lots of data, and we know something about what data is and how to think about it, but our exploration of data is not yet complete until we examine the context where we interact with and use data. For this we need to look at "data culture." What do we mean by this? In 2015, P. Ramaswamy* defined data culture as

the principle established in the process of social practice in both public and private sectors which requires all staff and decision-makers to focus on the information conveyed by the existing data and make decisions and changes according to these results instead of leading the development of the company based on experience in the particular field.

---

* P. Ramaswamy, 2015, How to Create a Data Culture (PDF). *Cognizant*, https://www.cognizant.com/InsightsWhitepapers/how-to-create-a-data-culture-codex1408.pdf, accessed August 26, 2018.

This is a rather limited definition as it focuses on data-driven decision-making as opposed to experiential and/or conceptual decision-making. Culture, in the context of data or, in fact, in any context is much broader than that. We need several additional concepts in order to define this broader definition.

The first of these is data appreciation. Data appreciation starts not strictly with the *data* but with what the data tells us. Most people are not mathematicians or data scientists so expressing the explanation of a result set as:

$$a = \frac{(\Sigma y)(\Sigma x^2) - (\Sigma x)(\Sigma xy)}{n(\Sigma x^2) - (\Sigma x)^2}^* \qquad a = -1.003$$

$$b = \frac{n(\Sigma xy) - (\Sigma x)(\Sigma y)}{n(\Sigma x^2) - (\Sigma x)^2} \qquad b = 0.362$$

$$r = \frac{n\Sigma xy - (\Sigma x)(\Sigma y)}{\sqrt{n(\Sigma x^2) - (\Sigma x)^2}\sqrt{n(\Sigma y^2) - (\Sigma y)^2}}^\dagger \qquad r = 0.694$$

This is not very helpful. *a* and *b* are the generalized equations for linear regression, a statistical technique used in almost all comparative quantitative analysis including the development of machine learning algorithms. Regression determines the (linear, in this case) relationship between a dependent and independent variable. In other words, given the value of the independent variable can we predict the value of the dependent variable? *r* is the linear correlation coefficient. Correlation shows us how well our prediction (regression) fits our data. Regression and correlation are familiar to almost all people who work with data, but there are much more effective ways to present the results and interpretation of these analyses than the generalized equations.

One of the best ways to do this is through stories. Large-scale data analysis is a story about the relationships and patterns

---

* http://www.statisticshowto.com/probability-and-statistics/regression-analysis/find-a-linear-regression-equation/, accessed August 30, 2018.
† https://mathbits.com/MathBits/TISection/Statistics2/correlation.htm

between things and how one set of measurements may influence another. These stories can be quite compelling and so representing analysis as a story about the data being analyzed can be a very effective way of getting and maintaining peoples' attention as well as influencing them. Here's an example:

A colleague and I published a paper* several years ago on a project that deployed contemporary analytics (Hadoop-based analytic stack with massive parallel Structured Query Language (SQL) execution, R integration, and a visualization tool) into community health centers (CHCs) in order to demonstrate both the difference between this approach and normal business intelligence and reporting tools, to train the CHC staff in the use of these tools and to produce some clinical and population analyses as examples. The data set of the largest participant covered more than 40 clinics and approximately 1 million patients. I have used this data set in the following example.

We know that the occurrence of Type 2 diabetes is comorbid with (tied to) the occurrence of a number of other health conditions. An analysis of this data consisting of pairwise linear regressions was executed with the following variables using Type 2 diabetes as the dependent (predicted) variable: hypertension, obesity, and heart disease (mainly congestive heart failure). The following tables show the significant results of this analysis.

| | | Diabetes | Hypertension | Obesity | Heart disease |
		Column 1	Column 2	Column 3	Column 4
Diabetes	Column 1	1			
Hypertension	Column 2	0.69371836	1		
Obesity	Column 3	–0.0669854	–0.0070465	1	
Heart disease	Column 4	0.48024104	0.5806169	–0.0972237	1

* D.J. Hartzband and F. Jacobs, 2016, Deployment of Analytics into the Healthcare Safety Net: Lessons Learned. *Online Journal of Public Health Information.*

Diabetes-Hypertension

	Coefficients	Standard Error	t Statistic
Intercept	−1.0035716	1.69360374	−0.5925658
X Variable 1	0.36245428	0.07111678	5.09660676

Diabetes-Heart Disease

	Coefficients	Standard Error	t Statistic
Intercept	0.92432045	0.27228486	3.39468174
X Variable 1	0.09402055	0.03245277	2.89715062

Heart Disease-Hypertension

	Coefficients	Standard Error	t Statistic
Intercept	13.1355989	2.74092694	4.79239292
X Variable 1	5.67617916	1.50420207	3.7735483

OK – this is slightly better than the generalized equations, (if you are a data geek) but even this is not much help. How about a story?

Emily is a 54-year-old African American woman who visited the health center complaining that she felt very light-headed in the mornings and that she had pains in her lower legs and feet. She was given a complete work-up and her random plasma glucose was 344 mmol/dl. At the time, her blood pressure was measured as 194/160. Her height was measured as 5' 3" and her weight as 188 lbs (body mass index (BMI) = 33.3). She was asked if she had ever been diagnosed with diabetes and told the physician's assistant that she had not been to a doctor in some time.

The health center had recently looked at their population and done a series of analyses to try to determine the most common comorbidities among their patients. They knew that Type 2 diabetes was associated with hypertension in their population (see above analysis) and that hypertension was associated with heart health. So they did further testing and interviewing with Emily to determine that she most probably had suffered a cardiac incident 3 months prior to her visit. She was counseled on diabetes and heart disease and put on a medication regimen. The combination of good medical practice and population analysis of a specific, local data set proved to be very important for Emily. This narrative, along with the analytic results, can give us a full picture of the analysis, how it was done, and what the results were.

There are several other ways of presenting the results of analyses as well as providing a better understanding of the analysis and results. Two of these are presenting the results in the context of a solution to a well-known problem and the use of games to enhance the understanding of the analysis and results. I'm not going to give examples of these techniques except to say that, in general, the connection of a fact or means of generating a fact is much more immediately grasped when associated with a solution to a known problem. The same is true when analytic methods and results are embedded in competitive games.*

Data appreciation is the understanding that data and the use of data in the analysis of various types as well as the results of these analyses are important in our everyday lives. We may be data scientists in our everyday lives (some of us actually are), or most probably (0.9999) we are not (couldn't resist). Even if we are not, we can and should appreciate not only the importance of data but also how its use can inform our decisions and planning in ways that simple experience cannot.

> **Awareness** – Knowledge or understanding of a situation or subject at the present time based on information or experience (*Cambridge English Dictionary*)

---

* S. Cooper, et al., 2010, Predicting Protein Structures with a Multiplayer Online Game. *Nature*, August 5, 466(7307): 756–760 (a paper by nine University of Washington authors and 57,000 FoldIt players).

Data appreciation is necessary for all people, regardless of whether they work directly with data or not. It is what allows us to have a general understanding of the importance of data in our lives and work – to have a context for the role that data plays "in the real world" (of course data plays just as important in the virtual world). Data awareness is the extension of this context to people who actually work with data. It is a set of skills that includes: a) what data is available and relevant to a specific problem; b) where the data is located and how to access it; c) what analytic techniques are in general appropriate for the data/problem set; and d) having a context for interpreting the results of the analysis. Data awareness is essential for data analysts, but it is also important for a whole range of people playing different roles – especially in healthcare. Some of these might include C-suite personnel. such as the chief financial officer or the chief medical officer. Many healthcare organizations now also have a chief medical information officer, sometimes in addition to a chief information officer. Many clinical providers also perform analysis or interact with analytic efforts in the course of treatment planning, treatment, and patient interaction.

Data as Culture

Organizations of all kinds have culture. Culture can be defined as: "the set of shared attitudes, values, goals, and practices that characterizes an institution or organization."*. Healthcare organizations have cultures. Much of the work on culture in healthcare organization recently has been focused on fostering a "culture of patient safety."† While safety is a very important

---

* https://www.merriam-webster.com/dictionary/culture
† S. Singer et al., 2003, Workforce Perceptions of Hospital Safety Culture. *Health Services Research*, 42(5): 1999–2021. https://www.ncbi.nlm.nih.gov/pmc/articles/PMC2254575/

part of culture in healthcare organizations, it is only one aspect. The practice of healthcare is in rapid transition today from a focus on the provision of services and the payment and reimbursement to doctors, hospitals, and healthcare organizations in general, to a focus on the provision of value, as measured by outcome and a variety of other indicators. Payment, reimbursement, etc. are now transitioning to value-based payments. My own experience of the culture of the healthcare organizations I have worked with has shown me that there is a deep tension at the heart of healthcare culture. This tension can be characterized as the very profound motivation of doctors and other healthcare providers to treat patients and realize the best possible outcome for those in their care versus the need of healthcare organizations to sustain themselves (for non-profit organizations) and to generate a profit (in for-profit organizations). (See Figure 3.1.)

I have done several large information technology transition projects in healthcare organizations in the past several years and have had to plan and execute cultural evolution projects

Figure 3.1   Semantic map for data culture.*

* Generated with Gephi 0.9.2, text source proprietary project report.

as well as technology projects to affect the transitions. Several of these projects were much less than successful because of the cultural aspects. I have developed a set of "do's and don'ts" with respect to building and facilitating a data culture in these organizations. These lists, along with my experiences on these projects, follow.

When building or facilitating a data culture in a healthcare organization, *do*:

a. Promote data appreciation and awareness throughout the organization
b. Elicit executive support (CEO and staff) in the planning and execution of data projects
c. Have data champions surface organically from the organization
d. Work to align the use of data with organizational strategy
e. Use cross-group collaboration to plan and interpret analytic results
f. Ensure that the information technology infrastructure can support the planned projects and/or ongoing data operations, and
g. Evaluate success based on the accomplishment of agreed-upon strategic goals

Similarly, when building or facilitating a data culture in a healthcare organization, *do not*:

a. Allow group agenda and lack of collaboration to subvert data appreciation and awareness
b. Commit to a specific technology or application before strategic goals are defined
c. Appoint program and project leads based on the existing hierarchy
d. Make the development of measures (key performance indicators, KPIs) the first (or second …) priority

e. Base the success of the program or project on the evaluation of KPIs
f. Delegate the development of a data culture to an outside entity (except as a consultant to organizational management)

Several years ago, I was engaged with a relatively large healthcare organization (about 90 clinics, 600+ providers, and over a million patients). The project was the evolution of their organization, in order to introduce an analytics practice into the clinical and IT groups. This project touched every part of the organization and included technology as well as organizational and cultural change efforts. There was a good deal of complicated technological work involved, but the most complicated work, and the biggest impediment to the project, was the organizational culture. There were several aspects of this. The CEO of the organization said all the right things when the project kicked off and was very cordial to me, but then did almost nothing to support the project and appointed a person on their staff to manage it internally who actually already had a full-time job as the vice president of programs and then as chief operations officer. There were several people on the executive staff of the organization who openly opposed this effort, including the director of IT who resigned several months after the project started, and the "personal assistant" to the CEO, who, while not actually on the organization chart, had a substantial amount of influence. It was close to impossible to overcome the opposition of these leaders without very strong support from the CEO. The lack of support for the concepts of data appreciation and data awareness, not to mention the extreme resistance to change in most of the internal groups that these influential managers evidenced, ensured that the people working for them did not embrace these ideas, and this, in turn, ensured that a data culture was difficult if not impossible to develop.

In addition, the culture of the organization was very insular and personal. Managers had their "territory" and did not want to see changes that would affect how they ran their groups. Part of this was reflected in a lack of collaboration between groups. There were very well-established silos that were difficult to breach. One exception was that the clinical and IT teams started having joint meetings to review technology requests and discuss project status. This was a high point in the overall project, but it happened because of the efforts of two non-management staff, one in each group, who started meeting to improve the effectiveness of IT requests, and then included more and more people until most of both groups were involved. These meetings ended when a new IT director, who did not see the value of them, was hired. All of these issues could have been addressed by strong support from the CEO.

The graphic at the beginning of this section (see Figure 3.1) is a semantic map of concepts related to "data culture." It shows that data awareness and executive support are the two most important criteria for developing a data culture, with data appreciation and organizational issues not far behind. It also shows data quality directly related to data awareness and collaboration separately but directly to both data appreciation and data awareness. This model of data culture is derived from a textual analysis of the extensive (proprietary) project report of the referenced analytics and organizational evolution project, but it seems to me to be more generally appropriate as a way of thinking about data culture. In this sense data culture is the overall set of structures, formal and informal rules/guidelines, technologies, attitudes, and practices present in an organization that refer directly or indirectly to data. The most important characteristics in the formation and reduction to practice of this culture are the development and presence of data awareness and data appreciation, the level of executive support for these attitudes, and the alignment of organizational structures and patterns of operation with data awareness and appreciation.

Data in Culture

This topic could be a book all on its own; in fact Amazon (April 2018) lists over 7000 book titles for a search on "data and society" with such titles as: *All Data are Local: Thinking Critically in a Data Driven Society*, *The Politics and Policies of Big Data: Big Data, Big Brother*, or *The Data Gaze: Capitalism, Power and Perception*. So much of our current information comes from new electronic data sources, social media being the most prominent, that we seem to be adrift on a sea of data and information with few guidelines or maps for structuring how we experience this tsunami or how we interpret it. Getting overwhelmed is easy ... much of the writing so far on this topic – not just books, but endless blogs, electronic newsletters, electronic news outlets, etc. – is slightly to definitely dystopian regarding this huge set of resources. If we step back, however, and look at those areas in our lives and our larger culture that are being influenced, some would say restructured, by the availability of this data, we can begin to see some patterns and maybe make some sense of the big data picture.

Some time ago the *Telegraph* newspaper published an article* that puts this in perspective. It's worth looking in some detail at the categories they pointed out as being affected by the rush of data. These are certainly not the only areas affected, but I think they are some of the more important ones. We can start with society in general. Society in general – so much of the information we see and use today, for almost every purpose, comes in the form of data from electronic sources that we could say that these media structure our society and our culture by providing selective and/or biased data. Of course, people also limit the data outlets they get information from, but this also structures society and culture. A recent

---

* https://www.telegraph.co.uk/technology/7963311/10-ways-data-is-changing-how-we-live.html

Pew Center for Journalism and Media survey* found that
78% of Americans aged 18–49 get some or all of their news
from social media sites; while for the first time over 50% of
Americans (55%) aged over 55 get the news from social media.
These percentages have increased since the study was done in
September 2017. So much has been written on the influence of
data on our society that it would be impossible to cover all of
the different aspects.† The following topics are selected from
the *Telegraph* article for some specific comments.

- Personal relationships‡ – There are currently over 7500
  dating sites worldwide; more than 1500 in the United
  States. Twenty percent of all committed relationships start
  online. Forty-nine million people worldwide have tried
  online dating and the revenue from the industry (2017) is
  thought to be about $1.8 billion. This is serious money.
  On the other hand, a large number of people using
  these sites fabricate some or all of their dating profile.
  About 20% of women use a picture from when they were
  younger and 40% of men lie about their jobs. Age matters, as 27% of users are age 18–24, with the percentage
  of users going down in each age group until only 3% of
  users are over 65. Data sites are not the only use of data
  in relationships. There is an almost universal use of both
  email and messaging once a connection has been made.
  Suffice to say that dating and relationships have been
  quite substantially changed by the advent of online data.
- Business operations – Almost every business, even Mom
  and Pop corner stores, are run using electronic applications. Segments of the economy as disparate as healthcare
  and aerospace manufacturing use electronic records and

---

* http://www.journalism.org/2017/09/07/
  news-use-across-social-media-platforms-2017/
† A Google search (October 26, 2018) produced 502,000,000 results on this and
  related topics.
‡ https://www.datingadvice.com/online-dating/online-dating-statistics

communication tools as well as, in the case of manufacturing, electronic design and process management tools
that were not available 15–20 years ago. In healthcare,
electronic workflows are necessary to keep the provision
of care organized. Electronic supply chains in all segments have made businesses more efficient and allowed
the sourcing of materials and services from previously
unavailable sources. It is difficult to underestimate how
the availability of data has affected business operations
and this is before we even mention the Internet of Things
and big data. Again, a huge amount has been written
about data transforming business.*

There are many other topics that could be covered here but
will not be. Here are just a few of them.

- Politics
- Education
- Shopping and commerce
- Maps and geoanalysis
- Advertising

William Gibson famously said, "The future is already here. It's
just not evenly distributed."† Unfortunately, the same is true of
data, it's here (there, everywhere), it's just not evenly distributed. Neither is data awareness and appreciation. This is one
of the causes of many of the inequalities in our society. The
advent of this huge amount of data has already changed our
society. Just as the productive use of data in an organization
depends on the development of the skills of data appreciation and data awareness, so too does the productive use of
data in society. The support and direction of leadership in an

---

* https://www.mckinsey.com/business-functions/mckinsey-analytics/our-insights/
achieving-business-impact-with-data
† Interview, *Fresh Air*, National Public Radio, August 31, 1993.

organization are necessary for the development of these data skills in an organization and in society. A society will take its attitudes about data appreciation, awareness, and use from its leaders, so their data-based activity is critically important. Finally, we have seen that data skills are a prerequisite for data quality. Without the emphasis on training in and leadership examples of these skills, a society is likely to produce and use data of limited quality, and use that data in non-optimal ways.

Chapter 4

Data Quality

What Is Data Quality?

The ISO 9000:2015* definition of data quality would be "data quality can be defined as the degree to which a set of characteristics of data fulfills requirements."[†] Remember that *data means facts that are verifiable,* so how does this definition align with the idea of quality. Let's explore the idea of quality first.

There are many attempts to determine the one list of data characteristics that should be used in this definition of quality. The one I have found to work best for healthcare data, and that I am currently using, is from Cai and Zhu.[‡] They propose five dimensions of data quality and characteristics for each dimension. The dimensions they describe are availability, usability, reliability, relevance, and presentation quality. For instance, if we look at the dimension of reliability, we see that the proposed characteristics are: accuracy, integrity, consistency, completeness, and auditability. These meet our sniff

---

* https://en.wikipedia.org/wiki/ISO_9000
† https://en.wikipedia.org/wiki/Data_quality
‡ L. Cai and Y. Zhu, 2015, The Challenges of Data Quality and Data Quality Assessment in the Big Data Era. *Data Science Journal*, 14:2: 1–10. doi:http://dx.doi.org/10.5334/dsj-2015-002

test (or at least mine) of how reliability might be characterized. If we then had definitions for how to measure each of these characteristics, we could produce an integrated measure of reliability for a specific data set. (See Figure 4.1.)

I deliberately chose reliability as this first example because each of the characteristics proposed can be measured (with the possible exception of integrity), that is, each can produce facts as a consequence of examination. Not all of Cai and Zhu's dimensions are so clean in this manner, but I'll take that up shortly. The question now becomes, "how are we to produce and evaluate these facts?" Let's start with reliability ...

The characteristics of data reliability according to Cai and Zhu (op. cit.) are accuracy, integrity, consistency, completeness, and auditability. Each of these can, to a certain extent, be measured. These measurements produce the facts or data that we are concerned with. As a trivial example we can measure the random plasma glucose in a person's blood. This is done through the use of a glucometer, which uses glucose oxidase on a test strip that an electrical current is passed through, and is then read as a concentration of glucose in the blood (in units of mg/dl). This measurement produces a fact (e.g. 120 mg/dl), which is the datum we are seeking. This fact is verifiable by taking multiple measurements. We might have two measurements a day for 30

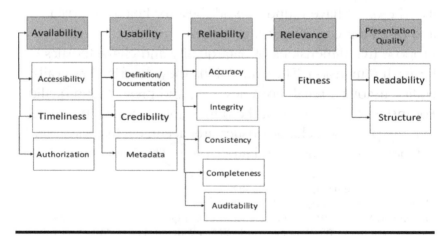

Figure 4.1   Data quality framework.

days (60 measurements), which constitutes a set of data for random plasma glucose for a specific patient.

OK, so is this data "reliable"? To answer (in the sense of Cai and Zhu, or really in general) we need to determine the status of the data with respect to the characteristics of reliability we have agreed on. First, how accurate is this data? Accuracy is generally taken to be the degree of closeness of a measurement to the entities true value.* This definition presupposes that we can: a) measure the entity in question and record the measurement in a standard set of units; b) know, by some means, the actual or true value of the entity at the time of the measurement; and c) compare the measurements or sets of measurements and determine the similarity between them.

In the case of random plasma glucose, for example, we can measure the quality and record the result in a standard set of units (mg/dl). We could, by separate and much more complicated means, determine the actual concentration of glucose in the blood at the time of the measurements, but this is seldom, if ever, done. Given that we do not have the actual or true values for our measurements, we cannot compare our measurements with the true values in order to be able to characterize the differences and determine the accuracy of our measurements. In order to have some idea of the measurement's accuracy, we need to be able to compare our results to an analog of the true value. This can be done in a number of ways:

a. We could compare them to an older (or possibly newer) set of values that were measured in the same way under the same circumstances (including discernible changes in the health or physical status of the patient).
b. We could compare them to a separate data source derived from the same measurements. In healthcare, this could be from insurance claims data, from a physician's notes on the patient, or from several other independent sources.

---

* https://en.wikipedia.org/wiki/Accuracy_and_precision

c. We could compare them by inference with a different set of measurements of the same characteristic (concentration of blood glucose) such as HbA1c measurements. HbA1c is a measure of average blood glucose (as a percentage) over time, usually 3 months. If your HbA1c measurement is 12.2, you are unlikely to have random plasma glucose in the non-diabetic range, so an inference can be made about the accuracy of the blood glucose measurements.

d. Finally, we could use a measure of accuracy of the test we are tracking as an analog of accuracy in our measurements. For instance, if the manufacturer's testing of the device (glucometer) we are using is that it is 99.3% accurate, we can assume that our data is in that range of accuracy.

Accuracy can be characterized statistically either by comparing the two sets of data to determine statistical similarity or by comparing statistics such a mean, standard error, etc. to determine similarity. If the two data sets are statistically similar, then the accuracy is high and can be represented by the probability levels of the test.

Is this data consistent? Consistency in this context has two dimensions. The first is syntactic, or content-based, consistency, and the second is semantic, or context-based, consistency. Content-based consistency is measured by comparing the same measurement that is recorded several times (perhaps in different places) to make sure that the values are similar. This appears to be the same as one measure of accuracy but in a different context. If different instantiations of the same data are similar (or identical), we can say that the data is consistent on a content basis.

Context-based consistency is dependent on the similarity of values of the same data measured for different purposes. Such data are often recorded in different places. An example would be a measurement of total cholesterol taken during a diabetic episode of 238 mg/dl and a measurement of total cholesterol taken a week later during a screening for cardiac disease of 164 mg/dl. These readings would not be consistent as they are in different clinical ranges for risk from cholesterol and taken quite close together. I'll cover the types of data issues and how they might be ameliorated in the next section.

Completeness is a measure that in healthcare is primarily directed at missing data. We can never really know if the data that we have on a patient is complete, but we can know that every time the patient was examined, specific values were measured. If we have random plasma glucose and total cholesterol values for all of a patient's visits to the doctor, then we have complete data for these characteristics (yes, I know that a doctor's visit may not actually mean seeing a doctor but possibly a nurse practitioner (certified registered nurse practitioner), a registered nurse, physician's assistant, or other provider).

Auditability is the ability of an auditor, human or algorithmic, to achieve accuracy in the verification of data held by a healthcare organization. Such audits are related to overall data quality in that the audit itself measures aspects of quality (accuracy, consistency, completeness, etc.), and this evaluation is auditable based on the difficulty of carrying it out. A data quality evaluation that is quite difficult due to missing data, incorrect data, and other anomalies is less auditable than one in which these issues are not impediments (see section on data issues in this chapter). Auditability can be improved by addressing such data anomalies and by following data governance practices that can minimize the introduction of data issues into the healthcare data set (see section on data governance in this chapter).

Data integrity is the maintenance, and the assurance, of the accuracy and consistency of data over its entire life cycle and is a critical aspect of the design, implementation, and usage of any system that stores, processes, or retrieves data.* Integrity, in this sense, is a composite or synthetic characteristic that is

---

* https://en.wikipedia.org/wiki/Data_integrity

composed of the other characteristics that make up reliability in the Cai and Zhu framework. As such it is a mainly subjective measure that we perceive according to our evaluation of the other characteristics in this dimension. Integrity is high when our measurements of accuracy, completeness, consistency, and auditability are high. If any of these measurements are low, our perception of integrity is correspondingly lower. Integrity can, therefore, be taken as a surrogate for our understanding of data reliability.

What about characteristics of other dimensions in this framework? There are measurable characteristics in both the availability and usability dimensions. Availability has accessibility and timeliness characteristics. Accessibility has several characteristics itself including (but not limited to) locatability, recoverability, and authorization. Locatability has to do with to what extent the specific data is findable. In order to be findable, you need to be able to describe the data you are looking for in enough detail that it is possible to find it, usually with a search engine. The workings of search engines are a major topic in themselves, but it is enough to say that most search engines operate by some form of syntactic matching. That is, they try to match the words in your description with content that they have indexed for discovery. In most cases, this matching is done on the basis of key word matching or matching of phrases or other (close to) exact similarities. If I search for data availability (Google, October 30, 2018: 0914), I get 533,000,000 results with only the first 20 or so being relevant. This is a microcosm of the issues in data availability itself. The system located a very large number of potential results, but we do not know how many of these results are recoverable. Many, in fact, the majority, may not be, due to broken and/or missing links.

Timeliness is also important here. Many of these links are years old and, even if they are recoverable, they may no longer be relevant. They might have aged out in terms of their content being superseded or their source losing its credibility.

It's necessary to realize, though, that just because a fact (or the exposition of a set of facts such as in an academic paper) is "old," it may still be relevant and important in the context of the inquiry. In formal logic, for instance, the work that Kurt Gödel* published in 1931 is still relevant and important today.

Usability has one characteristic that is measurable and that is its definition. Many issues with the accuracy and interpretation of data are related to problems with the definition of data terms (see section later in this chapter on data issues).

Finally, of increasing importance in today's data environments, the whole question of authorization including data security, privacy, encryption, etc. is a primary focus. From a quality perspective, security is more related to getting the right data to the right people than it is to privacy. Data could be of high quality (accurate, timely, consistent, complete, etc.), but could be made available to the wrong people or programs, which would be a privacy violation. An authorized user, that is one with appropriate credentials to access the data, could make an improper secondary distribution that would also be a violation of privacy. These dimensions (authorization/security vs. privacy) appear to be orthogonal with respect to quality.

The question of relevance comes up independently as well. Relevance appears to be a subjective category, that is that people (and even systems) may differ on the degree of relevance of a fact or set of facts, but relevance is related to a number of characteristics that are measurable, such as definition. A fact may be irrelevant because its referent is the wrong definition. There are many reasons why this might be the case. The definition might just be wrong, or the wrong measures might be used (milliliters vs. deciliters), etc. Whatever the case, inappropriate or misutilized definitions will affect the relevance of data.

---

* K. Gödel, 1931, Über formal unentscheidbare Sätze der Principia Mathematica und verwandter Systeme, I. *Monatshefte für Mathematik und Physik*, vol. 38, no. 1, pp. 173–198.

The characteristics of reliability also affect relevance. Data that is inaccurate, inconsistent, or incomplete will be of low or even no relevance depending on the degree of error exhibited.

When people think of data quality, they often think of those measurable qualities associated with data reliability and usability. The more subjective qualities may be acknowledged but are usually not included in technical discussions of quality.

The Cai and Zhu framework is only one way of looking at quality. Wang and Strong* present another framework that is illustrated below. It is presented for comparison and to indicate that most frameworks currently influencing thinking on data quality are similar enough to be seen as equivalent. (See Figure 4.2.)

A comparison of these two frameworks shows that even though their primary dimensions are quite different, the underlying characteristics of data quality are very similar. Many of the underlying characteristics are identical, and those

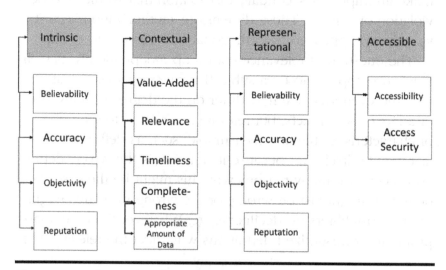

Figure 4.2   Alternative data quality framework.

---

* D.Y. Wang and D.M. Strong, 1996, Beyond Accuracy: What Data Quality Means to Data Consumers. *Journal of Management Information Systems*, 12(4): 5–34.

that aren't are close enough to be equivalent. This tells us that, even though data quality has been looked at in many different ways, there is a consensus around the underlying objective and subject criteria for assessing data quality.

Data Issues and What Can Be Done about Them?

Several years ago, a colleague and I published a paper* on a project that deployed a contemporary, Hadoop-based† analytic stack into the information technology infrastructure at a number of community health centers (CHCs) and primary care associations (PCAs). Part of the project was an initial data quality evaluation of data held in either the CHCs' electronic health record (EHR) systems or in a data warehouse or extract of data derived from the EHR systems. This evaluation was based on a process that was developed called Level-Up. Level-Up is a comparative analytic exercise that was meant to evaluate demographic and clinical data in different repositories derived from the same source. It was initially to serve as a means to align the data in the EHR system, or a data extract/warehouse derived from it, with the data in an analytic stack. The Level-Up exercise consisted of executing a number of defined queries in both systems. The CHC IT staff performed this set of queries on their EHR or data extract, using the definitions that the CHC staff used in their reporting, and the RCHN CHF (Community Health Foundation) director of technology research performed the set of queries on the analytic stack using the standardized uniform data system (UDS) data

---

* D.J. Hartzband and F. Jacobs, 2016, Deployment of Analytics into the Healthcare Safety-Net: Lessons Learned. *Online Journal of Public Health Informatics*, 5(3): e205.
† https://hadoop.apache.org/

definitions.* The results were then compared and differences in data definitions as well as data quality problems, such as missing data, out-of-range data, unusable data, etc., were identified. The queries used included:

- Number of patients served per year
- Number of patients served presenting with specific diagnoses, including hypertension, diabetes, obesity, heart disease, and behavioral health conditions
- Rank order of prevalent comorbidities[†]
- Cost per patient, per year[‡]
- Cost, per comorbidity, per year

The results of this analysis revealed several types of potential data quality issues as defined and discussed above. Although the nature and extent of the problems varied across sites, the problems – including definitional conflicts, conversion issues, and structural challenges – were not unique to any site and, to some extent, were evident at all sites. Table 4.1 summarizes the most common types of data anomalies found and gives some suggestions for ameliorating these issues (where possible).

While seven data issues were identified in the EHR data from the participating CHCs, five of these errors are related to data entry problems. These include:

- Deviation from standard or agreed upon definitions – Data that is entered according to purely local and/or idiosyncratic definitions is usually inconsistent, even

---

* UDS definitions (Health Resources and Services Administration, HRSA, and Department of Health and Human Services, HHS) are used for all terms including: visits, patients, conditions, and diagnoses. http://www.bphcdata.net/docs/uds_rep_instr.pdf

[†] Data quality and access issues prevented the accurate calculation of comorbidities. (P2A)

[‡] Actual cost (expenditure), not billed cost (revenue) – It is important to note that actual cost was not able to be calculated at any of the health centers and so these queries were not run. (P2A)

internally, and cannot be shared or aggregated for analysis. Definitions most often found in the study to be in
error were for the terms patient and encounter. The
study also found that often UDS-based diagnosis lists
(International Classification of Diseases, ICD, codes) were
not used to report on specific conditions.

■ Missing and/or omitted data – Such data is often not
recoverable.
■ Incorrectly entered data.
■ Data not entered into searchable field – There are many
reasons for this. Often data is entered inconsistently into
one of several fields, or data is imported as text (into
some form of physician or administrative notes) and so
cannot be easily recovered by query.

Table 4.1   Data Issues and Possible Corrections

Data Issue	Possible Solutions	Comments
1. Deviation from standard definitions	Remediate using standard definitions	UDS definitions used for all reports and analysis
2. Missing and/or omitted data	Attempt to recover data from other sources	Claims data, provider notes, site logs, etc.
3. Incorrectly entered data	As in 2	Development of data awareness may help
4. Data values not entered into searchable field	Natural language application may assist	Often from imported data
5. Errors related to structured/ complexity of EHR	Simplify workflows for data capture, work with vendor to improve EHR	Easier to correct data at capture than at clinical use or analysis
6. Errors related to migration of EHR system	Maintain original database for report gen and quality	Work with vendor(s) to ensure correct migration
7. Errors related to cultural or organizational bias	Work to uncover bias, process to advise staff	Progress must be reviewed

■ Structural and functional complexity and/or ambiguity of EHR complicates data entry – Many EHRs have multiple places to enter the same data as well as multiple tabs and clicks to get to specific data. This substantially increases the possibility of incorrect data entry.

The remaining errors found in the study were related either to product migration issues or cultural and/or organizational biases.

Correcting these issues falls into several general categories of actions:

■ Agree on standard definitions and, where relevant, use UDS definitions for CHCs or other standard definitions (from professional college or association).
■ Review current data entry process for complexity and ambiguity.
■ Redesign data entry process if necessary.
■ Retrain personnel, if necessary, to ensure that standard definitions are used.
■ Recover missing, omitted, or incorrectly entered data from alternative sources such as claims and billing data, provider notes, site logs, etc.
■ Recover data in non-searchable fields, perhaps from a review of notes or other text fields.
  – Natural language capabilities might also be used to recover such data, although mapping data values into appropriate fields is often a challenge.
■ Ameliorate errors due to product migration by keeping a full backup of the pre-migration data and also keeping a license for at least one instance of the former EHR system so that the backup data is readable while the migration is being completed.

As the above elements suggest, data errors are complex and the steps required to address them are often laborious.

Correcting systemic and non-random issues in data quality is much easier at the point of data entry than at the point of data analysis or use by providers. Data entry processes, including both manual and automated processes, must be reviewed and redesigned, if necessary, to minimize the potential for introducing errors. It is essential to recognize and address bias in the organizational culture that might hamper such processes.

This material is presented not because this work was unique or seminal, but because the results in terms of types of data issues found in healthcare and especially EHR data are typical of results from other studies and recent surveys.* A recent study analyzing 9000 patient safety reports in pediatric settings found that in 36% of cases a medication event occurred and in 19% of these cases harm could have occurred.† In an interview, one of the study authors commented:

> when we say usability, what we're talking about is essentially how easy and intuitive it is for our clinicians to interact with and use electronic health records. And the finding is essentially that the poor usability of some of these electronic health records can actually impact the patient and can do so negatively. So, we're seeing patients being harmed potentially because of the design and use of these systems.‡

---

* https://www.healthcareitnews.com/news/biggest-ehr-challenges-2018-security-interoperability-clinician-burnout, https://www.omicsonline.org/open-access/electronic-health-record-management-expectations-issues-and-challenges-2157-7420-1000265.php?aid=90749
† https://www.healthaffairs.org/doi/abs/10.1377/hlthaff.2018.0699
‡ http://www.wbur.org/commonhealth/2018/03/27/ehr-design-patient-harm

Data Governance

Data governance, at its simplest, is the set of concepts, processes, and mechanisms that provides a standardized focus on data quality for an organization. A very substantial body of material has been generated on this topic in the past 10 years or so. A Google search using data governance as the keywords provided 195,000,000 results (in 0.36 seconds).* A good deal of this material has to do with models and frameworks for governance, many of which, at least to me, seem confusing, conflicting, or overly complex. Governance, as it is practiced currently, is most often centered around a governance committee that is responsible for deciding on the guidelines that make up an organization's data governance framework. Data stewards are then designated who are responsible for ensuring that these guidelines are carried out.

The areas that guidelines are developed in are the characteristics or criteria that make up the data quality frameworks we've already reviewed. These may include:

▪ Concept development for high-level quality dimensions (characteristics and criteria: e.g. privacy, accuracy, timeliness)
  – Description of concepts and their interrelationships
▪ Standardized definitions for all managed terms
  – Including both concepts, such as privacy, and detailed definitions of data terms, such as length of wing segment (aerospace) or blood pressure metric (healthcare)
▪ Processes to ensure the accuracy, consistency, timeliness, and completeness of data entry
  – Processes such as data pre-entry check for range specification, such as BMI < 100 (healthcare)
▪ Processes to ensure the continuity, reliability, and maintenance of the infrastructure that is used to manage data

---

* November 8, 2018: 13:54.

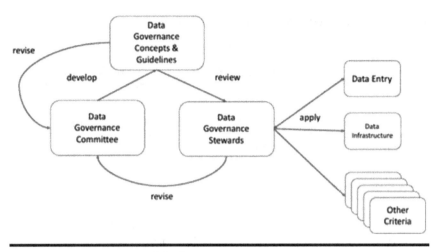

Figure 4.3   Process model, data governance.

   – Processes to review storage allocation and utilization, software maintenance schedules, and review processes, etc.
■ Processes to ensure the privacy and security of data
   – Regular privacy and security audits

Figure 4.3 is a schematic of the data governance process.

   In this governance model, the Data Governance Committee develops concepts and standards as described above. Data stewards then apply these standards to the criteria shown on the right-hand side of the figure. There are several feedback loops that ensure thorough review of both the concepts and standards and of the application of the same. Table 4.2* gives a more detailed list of criteria addressed.)

   I have been involved in several large- and medium-sized data governance efforts over time, one in aerospace, one in automotive manufacturing, and a more recent one in healthcare. The aerospace and automotive efforts were by very large corporations and were planned for multiple years of work

---

* In part from C. Bradley, 2013, https://www.slideshare.net/inforacer/
   impdata-gover/36

Table 4.2 Detailed Criteria for Data Governance

Business Criteria	Information Criteria	Technology Criteria
Risk	Management	Architecture
Finance	Quality	Security
Actuarial	Location	Integration
Marcom	Reporting	Access
Human resources (HR)	Analysis	Development

starting with data inventories and the development of a data dictionary for concepts and terms. The aerospace effort was called off after 2 years of work by a very talented committee of engineers, product specialists, manufacturing managers, and other specialists when they failed to deliver a data dictionary that was considered definitive. The work in automotive manufacturing was "completed," or at least the vice president in charge of the work declared it complete after a data dictionary was circulated and data stewards were tasked with ensuring that standardized terms were used in the design of information and manufacturing process management systems. In both cases, a large and well-intentioned effort failed to provide the necessary information and process definitions to apply to data governance.

The project in healthcare was done with an aggregation of clinics (about 70) that were geographically distributed across a large state and served about 1,000,000 patients in total a year. This group of clinics reported annually to the Department of Health and Human Services using a standardized set of measures and definitions specified by HHS and published yearly as guidelines. The data governance effort was greatly complicated by the fact that that many of the clinics used unique or idiosyncratic definitions, even though standard definitions for reporting to HHS were specified. Most of these clinics were reluctant and/or unwilling to give up their definitions so that decisions had to be made by a centralized group that were not always adhered to by the individual clinics. A common governance model was not possible under these circumstances.

In each of these cases, a well-intentioned and serious effort was made to develop a data governance program, and in each case the effort was less than successful. Why would this be the case and what can be done about it?

Issues in Data Governance and More Modern Approaches

It is very difficult to successfully provide data governance after the fact.

In both the aerospace and automotive cases, the project to provide data governance was started after the organizations had been doing data management for many years as part of their normal engineering processes, but had not attempted to move to formal data governance procedures until their information management processes were quite mature. In the aerospace case, governance was mandated for an aircraft manufacturing process that was already in place and where the bill-of-materials (BoM) for the aircraft in question had over 1,000,000 discrete parts, each of which was itemized in multiple BoMs, sometimes as many as 8–10 for the same aircraft (as-designed, as-ordered, as-built, as-maintained, as-modified, etc.). In fact, difficult is an understatement if you are attempting to define a data governance regime for data-driven projects of this size. This was, of course, only one of several aircraft projects of this size in the company, so that a company-wide governance environment becomes less and less possible.

The same was true of the effort(s) in automotive manufacturing. Each individual car has only about 30,000 parts,*

---

* According to NAPA (National Auto Parts Association). https://www.mnn.com/lifestyle/eco-tourism/sponsorphotos/11-fascinating-facts-about-cars/how-many-parts-must-a-car-have

although many more individual units are manufactured. General Motors, for instance, sold about 10,000,000 units worldwide in 2016* (a unique bill-of-materials is, however, not maintained for each car). Applying data governance to this amount of data that has already been categorized by several different organizations as challenging.† Each organization already has its processes for data standardization, data entry, quality assurance, hardware and software usage, etc. Unless there is a very strong central management group with the support from very senior management, and the authority to enforce governance standards, or even mandate participation in the governance effort, the project will be either a partial or a complete failure.

In healthcare, the issues are perhaps even more difficult. Here we are not dealing with building aircraft or automobiles, but with the data used in treating patients. Doctors are deeply committed to treating patients, it is basically the only reason (with some exceptions) that they put up with constantly evolving technology. It could be argued that building aircraft and automobiles is also about people's safety, but while this is a major design goal, it is not the single primary goal. Clinics and hospitals develop their own processes for dealing with data, usually with the motivation of making relevant data available to medical providers for treatment planning, point-of-care interaction, care continuity, etc. (as well as administrative and financial purposes). Once these processes are formed, it is very difficult to change them, regardless of the reason.

It is also true that many healthcare organizations, of all sizes and types, see themselves as unique – that is having a unique patient base and a unique approach to the treatment of those patients. This may result in unique data definitions, even

---

* https://money.cnn.com/2017/02/07/news/companies/gm-record-sales-profits/index.html

† This brings up the topic of data governance for ultra-large analytic data sets (big data) that will be addressed later in this chapter.

if standardized terms, workflows, and processes for dealing with data are already mandated by regulation and/or common practice. Some of this, and particularly the issues associated with data definition, were discussed in the previous section on data issues.

It seems as if the development and practice of a data governance program can be quite challenging, especially in healthcare environments where definitions and processes for handling data are already established and where a large body of data is under management. This is certainly true in my experience if we are dealing with the model of data governance that has been developed over the last 20–30 years, but the definition and practice of data governance are starting to change. Much of the focus has previously been on dealing with issues of compliance with regulations. The 2017 CIO Water Cooler Survey on Data Governance* found that only 39% of the organizations participating had developed a data governance framework in order to comply with regulatory requirements, while 54% stated that improving process efficiency was their primary goal. Fully 63% agreed with the statement "We want our data to be of good quality so that our company can achieve its strategy and objectives." Just as interesting is that the survey found that companies of two different sizes were currently implementing such programs – 100–499 employees and 10,000+ employees. This shows that organizations of all sizes, not just the largest ones, are implementing governance programs. Organizations increasingly are looking at data governance as a way to leverage data as a strategic asset.

This new approach is less formal in its structure and more flexible in terms of actual process management. It is, in part, a reaction to a) the requirements of determining and improving data quality in ultra-large (>1 terabyte, TB) data sets, and

---

* https://ciowatercooler.co.uk/research/data-governance-survey-2017/

b) the need to scale the resources necessary to perform governance in a wide range of organizations.

I've deferred the question of big data quality and governance until now. This is partly because big data, >1 terabyte in my definition, is one of the forcing factors changing what data quality and data governance mean. If we think of applying conventional data quality and governance models to ultra-large data sets, it quickly becomes evident that these methods are not adequate to provide data that is appropriate for analysis and exploration. The well-described characteristics of these data sets include a) ultra-large volume; b) extreme heterogeneity in both types of data and sources of data; and c) different, generally much shorter, turnover and life cycle of the data. With respect to volume, there is a very large difference between having 150,000 instances of a data definition from 3–4 different data sources, all of which are EHRs (3 years of data from the analytics project, 50,000 patients/year, 3 years for the definition of patient), then having 50–60 million instances of the same definition from 12–20 entirely different types of data sources. It is just not feasible to do a priori standardization of every instance when normalizing the data source. The same is true of any other conventional governance technique with this amount of data.

Data heterogeneity is a similar problem. If you are aggregating millions of records from very disparate data sources (EHRs, disease registries, lab systems, population data, social determinants data, macro- and microeconomic data, state and federal demographic and economic data, etc.), it is not possible to normalize the data in conventional ways (this will be discussed again in the section on HIT infrastructure evolution). Finally, if data is changing quickly, it is not worth the effort to normalize it in conventional ways. The pragmatic comparative issue resolution and governance technique described in the last section is an example of governance methods that are being proposed and used for ultra-large data sets.* Conventional data quality and governance techniques seek to provide a complete, end-to-end data source that is correct, standardized, and usable, often in one place, such as a data warehouse or extract. The emphasis is on correct data entry and data standardization before use. The new pragmatic consensus, not just for big data, emphasizes correct-as-possible data at the time of use and backcasting the analysis of data issues from identified anomalous results. Standardization of various kinds is often written into the data models used for specific analysis. This whole topic will be returned to when the evolution of HIT infrastructure is discussed in Chapter 6.

Practical Issues and Approaches in Data Quality

In the previous section on data issues, a data quality evaluation method called Level-Up was described. There are many pragmatic methods like this, but this is the one that I developed and know best, so I'll use it as the example in this section.

As already described, the first thing evaluated in the data analytics project was the reliability and accuracy of reports for a number of patients with specific diagnoses. These included hypertension, diabetes, obesity, and congestive heart disease. Data was from 30 clinics for the years 2012, 2013, and 2014. Total patients were 400,000 ± 20,000. Comparisons were made between data in a data warehouse aggregated by the Primary Care Association serving these 30 clinics and a data extract made into a massive parallel distributed file system aggregated by a contractor working with me. Both data sources were

---

* See D. Loshin, 2014, Understanding Big Data Quality for Maximum Information Usability. SAS Institute. https://www.sas.com/content/dam/SAS/en_us/doc/whitepaper1/understanding-big-data-quality-107113.pdf; B.J. Dooley, 2018, Data Quality Evolution with Big Data and Machine Learning; G. Firikin, 2017, Adapting Data Governance to Big Data. https://tdwi.org/articles/2017/04/14/adapting-data-governance-to-big-data.aspx. And many others.

derived from the databases underlying the clinics' electronic health record systems. Queries against the data warehouse were made by the PCA and queries against the file system were made by the contractor.

The first thing that we noticed was that the numbers reported for each diagnosis were quite different from each data store, in some cases by <1% but in some cases by >10%. This was the first indication that there could be a quality problem with the diagnosis data. The results of this comparison alerted us to work backward from the queries when there appeared to be a discrepancy. This is a general rule. Using a pragmatic comparative method (like Level-Up) to assess quality gives a starting point to work backward in order to analyze the possible data issue. In this case, it was found that the numbers in the underlying data stores were very similar, but that the definitions used to structure the queries were different in two specifics. The first was that the definition of patient used by the PCA was quite idiosyncratic, seemingly excluding a large number of people treated at the participating clinics as not patients. This was even though there is a standard definition for patient that the clinics are mandated (by HRSA and HHS) to use. The second was that the diagnoses were determined by lists of ICD-9 codes (data was from 2012–2014 so ICD-9 was still in force) and each clinic used different sets of codes to define the diagnoses. These definitional differences were discovered by working backward to examine the Structured Query Language (SQL) code used to execute the queries. Once the queries were rewritten using standard definitions, the differences in numbers of patients with each diagnosis were resolved.

It turns out that there was a second quantitative dimension that we could have worked backward along. This was the percentage of the patient population exhibiting each diagnosis. The Centers for Disease Control (CDC) publishes "QuickStats" every year that includes the percentage of certain diseases in the general population of the United States. We assumed that the patient populations would have higher percentages of these diagnoses than the general population, but in each case, they were lower. An example would be that the clinic population never had a percentage of diagnosed obesity of higher than 11% while the CDC reported that for the years in question the percentage of obesity in the general population was about 35%. Anecdotally, several chief medical officers at participating clinics related that they thought the percentage of obesity among their patients might be as high as 60–70%. This was a clear indication that something was wrong with the data. Again, working backward from this discrepancy showed us several things. The first was that the percentages in the study were correct – diagnoses of obesity in the clinics' patient populations did not exceed 11%. By questioning providers and chief medical officers in a number of the clinics, we found that providers did not report a diagnosis of obesity very often. There appeared to be several reasons, including a desire to not offend the patient and a cultural bias in the communities served that "larger" people were more attractive.

A final example is that we also saw a number of highly suspect values for body mass index (BMI) in the data, including several values in excess of 500. The largest BMI ever recorded (posthumously) was for Jon Brower Minnoch, who was 6′ 3″ and at one time weighed approximately 1400 pounds for a BMI of 175.* When the vendor of the EHR that held this data was asked about it, they said that it was impossible for these values to be entered as that specific field had a range associated with it. This was true, although there was no action associated with range violations.

These data issues had three different causes. In the case of the diagnosis percentages, there were two different nonstandard definitions used: the definition for patient and the ICD-9 code-based definition for the disease. In the case of low

---

* https://www.google.com/search?q=worlds+heaviest+manandie= utf-8andoe=utf-8andclient=firefox-b-1

obesity reporting, the low diagnoses percentages appeared
to be the result of both organizational and cultural biases.
Finally, in the BMI example, clearly incorrect data was entered.
In each of these cases, more thorough attention to the data
would have potentially corrected the issue at its origin. This
attention is what I've described as data appreciation and data
awareness (Chapter 3). Understanding the use of the data and
its importance in the strategy of the organization as well as
knowledge of what data is available, how it's acquired, and
how it's analyzed (and by whom) allows the people who are
entering and reviewing the data to catch many of the definitional and entry anomalies, such as missing or obviously incorrect data. Of course, there are data issues that are much more
difficult to identify at the entry and review stages. The obesity
anomaly provides an example. If the problem is in fact caused
by organizational and cultural bias, it would be very hard for
the people involved to identify problems in this category, as
they would share these biases. A deep focus on data appreciation and awareness may help even this cause of data problems
as it provides a focus on how the data is to be used, not simply
whether there is a value for the data.

Data governance is evolving from a relatively fixed set
of organizational structures and business processes focused
mainly on regulatory compliance to a much more flexible set
of structures and processes that emphasize data as an organizational asset aligned with broader strategy and goals. In
this sense, governance consists of a priori processes for things
like data entry and initial review, a posteriori processes for
comparative quality analysis that allow a backward working
perspective to identify and potentially ameliorate data anomalies, as well as flexible working group structures as needed
to plan and carry out these processes. This new form of data
governance is effective, but much less burdensome in both
effort and resources. It does, however, emphasize and require
a commitment to data appreciation and awareness at all levels
of an organization. (See Figure 4.4.)

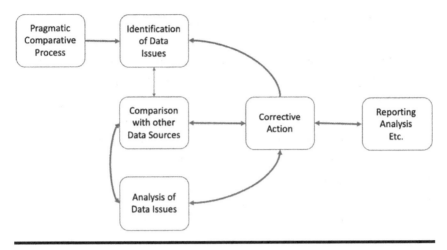

Figure 4.4 Pragmatic data governance process.

Data in Context

Big, Little, Right ...

I briefly touched on this in Chapter 2, What Is Data? Given the current emphasis on "big data" (see Chapter 5 on data analysis), the topic of data volume has become quite important. My personal experience has shown that most clinics (Federally Qualified Health Centers) today have about 10 gigabytes (GBs) of data in total. This includes clinical, administrative, and financial data. Primary Care Associations generally have 50–100 gigabytes, while medium-sized hospitals may have up to 5 terabytes. Many estimates are that the amount of health-care data is likely to grow at 40–60% a year, that is to double every 2 years. This implies that these organizations will have approximately 30 terabytes of information in 5 or so years, and that some organizations will have up to 100 terabytes. In comparison, the entire print collection of the Library of Congress is about 15 terabytes. What are the implications of this in technology and in strategy for healthcare organizations?

The first thing is that while data volume is often an issue in the sense that appropriate hardware and software is required to manage and use very large volumes of data, very large volumes of data are not always needed in order to perform effective and productive analysis. For many, if not most, analyses required for managing the delivery of healthcare today it is more a question of "right data" rather than big data. Right data is the data volume and content that is relevant to the question or questions that are being asked. Data volume is often limited by the specifics of data collection and data availability. For instance, if we are trying to determine trends in the treatment of pediatric asthma for a set of clinics, and each clinic has 4 years of data on between 2000 and 6000 patients, this would be a modest amount of data – perhaps in the range of 3–5 gigabytes. This is an amount of data that most current systems could analyze in memory. The fact that this is a small amount of data is immaterial so long as it is the right data and the right amount of data. Very few healthcare organizations have truly big data, NASA-size data – actually only NASA has NASA-size data – but as I have written here, even small clinics will be doubling the size of the data they need to take into account every 2 years, so data becomes big, fast.

The second thing related to data quality is that not all data anomalies result in an unusable data set. Depending on the type of data issue, it may be possible to recover data from other sources as needed or in many cases complete the analysis without the anomaly affecting the relevance of the outcome.

Of course, it's not just data volume that is increasing at a faster and faster rate. It's also the heterogeneity of the data, the rate of change of the data, and many other factors. I'll return to all this in Chapter 5, on data analysis.

Does Quality Matter?

This seems like an odd question to be asking after all this emphasis on data governance and the measurement of data quality. It is not, however, an idle question. There have been many papers published on this topic and a number of them have concluded that data quality may not matter as much, especially in the era of big data.* The tone of much of this material appears to be that quality, in the sense we've been writing about, will "even itself out" given enough data, that is enough data will be of usable quality that some percentage of unusable data will be acceptable. The problem with this assertion, however, is that even if the source is petabytes (PBs) of data, it still might not be usable if a large percentage of the data is missing or incorrect in any of the ways corresponding to the quality issues already defined. To have 50 PBs of data is not a panacea for data quality; in fact, it may be an issue in itself. How do you evaluate quality in 50 PBs of data? Is there a sampling technique that could give you an indication of overall data quality in data volumes such as this? Are there other and/or new measures of quality that will have to be taken into account? The bottom line is that quality does matter, regardless of whether you are working with 50 PBs or 5 GBs of data, and many of the same approaches to the measurement of quality can be scaled to work at both ends of the scale.

The criteria for data quality and data governance have been defined and refined over the last 25 years or so, but the advent of ultra-large (>1 PB) data sets requires us to re-examine these criteria. Loshin (2014)[†] provides a good summary of these changes, which include:

■ Multiple, heterogeneous sources – Data sets are often made up of different types of data, such as structured alphanumeric, unstructured document, unstructured

---

* See O. Kwon, N.Y. Lee, and B. Shin, 2014, Data Quality Management, Data Usage Experience and Acquisition Intention of Big Data Analytics. *International Journal of Information Management*, 34: 387–394. R.Y. Wang and D.M. Strong, 1996, Beyond Accuracy: What Data Quality Means to Data Consumers. *Journal of Management Information Systems*, 12(4): 5–33. B. Dooley, 2018, Data Quality Evolution with Big Data and Machine Learning. https://tdwi.org/articles/2018/05/04/diq-all-data-quality-evolution-with-big-data-and-machine-learning.aspx. And many more.
[†] D. Loshin, 2014, Understanding Big Data Quality for Maximum Usability. SAS Institute. https://www.sas.com/content/dam/SAS/en_us/doc/whitepaper1/understanding-big-data-quality-107113.pdf

non-document, image, or audio derived from sources outside your organizational control.

■ Lack of control of external sources – Aggregating and using data from such sources means that you and your organization did not have any control over data entry, data management (until it entered your system), data transformation (likewise), or any governance that may (or may not) have been applied. Data is aggregated into your system as it was in the source system, for better or for worse.

■ Different economics and technology for data management – The advent of technologies like the Hadoop Distributed File System (HDFS) and other similar large-scale distributed management platforms make it possible to acquire and store all the data from multiple sources and aggregate it with all the data from your own sources (EHR systems, practice management systems, financial and cost accounting systems, registries, project data systems, etc.). One consequence of this is that you do not need to expend time or resources on determining what data to keep – you just keep all of it.

■ Maintaining consistency – Much effort is currently spent on data cleansing. While this is essential for conventional data warehousing and governance, it severs the managed data from its external source. This can make many operations (like validation from original source) difficult or impossible.

■ Lack of semantics – As above, once the data is aggregated into the heterogeneous store, it loses its context. This means that interpretation of the data is situational, based on the use the data is put to rather than the context where it was collected and originally stored. This can result in the same data being interpreted in different ways, especially if it is used in different types of analysis. This may be a problem as data in large aggregations may be used in many different ways over time.

These different characteristics of ultra-large data sets require us to think differently about the meaning of data quality and the practice of data governance. I've already written on practical a posteriori approaches to data quality and governance. These types of approaches, focused on and designed with respect to the specific use of the data, may be the only appropriate way to deal with quality and governance in both modest-sized data sets (up to approximately 10 TBs), medium-sized (10 TBs to 1 PB), and "large" data sets (>1 PB). Steps to execute this type of governance include:

1. Identify data relevant to analysis and source of data
2. Design a set of initial queries to explore potential and/or suspected data issues, in part based on how data will be used (in analysis)
3. Review and interpret results of both exploratory and analytic queries to identify potential data quality issues
4. Determine if any corrective action is needed in order that analysis may be credibly completed and carry out corrective action if feasible
5. Maintain record(s) of exploratory results and corrective actions for future analyses and reference
6. Optionally develop models of analysis taking exploratory results and data issue interpretation into account

With respect to this last point, there are some results in logic and model theory that allow models to be developed, even if duplicate or contradictory data exists.

There are many reasons why duplicate rows in a conventional database are a problem. Many of these are operational, such as the generation of different keys for identical information, the need to store more information than necessary, issues with security and identity, etc. At a more fundamental level, if we think of data as verifiable facts that make up a model, then the answer to duplicate axioms or facts is simple. We know from Zermelo-Fraenkel (ZF) set theory that sets (first-order models conform to ZF set theory) do not have duplicate sentences (axioms, facts). We can show that:

> ***The set A = {1,1,1,2,2} is identical to the set
> B = {1,2} because one can show A ⊆ B and B ⊆ A
> and therefore A = B. Both have cardinality 2.****

Duplicate facts are not valid in our data models and so the methods that have been developed to identify and remove such entries are important for the validity of our data models. Please note that there are entities such as multisets (bags)† that do allow multiple identical entries. These are not elements of ZF set theory but can be used to form models. Also, please note that none of these entities are sequenced, that is order does not matter, which implies that:

1. {a,b} ≡ {b,a}, {a,a,b} ≡ {a,b} (in ZF)
2. mset{a,a,b} ≢ {a,b}, mset{a,a,b} ≡ mset{a,b,a}

Looking at our data models as bags or multisets, which is much more realistic than requiring that they conform to ZF set theory (or relational algebra for that matter‡), means that we need a theoretic means for dealing with duplicates

---

* https://math.stackexchange.com/questions/391516/
  cardinality-of-a-set-with-repeating-elements
† https://en.wikipedia.org/wiki/Multiset
‡ Relational algebra, proposed by E.F. "Ted" Codd of IBM in 1970, is a modified (constrained) set of set-theoretic operators that is consistent but not complete, for instance it cannot express transitive closure.

and contradictions in the data set. A contradiction can be
defined as:

S ∧ ~S → T (both S and the negation of S are true)
  Suchenek (1985, 1986) has shown:
Given:

1. $W \subset S$ *in F*
2. $I \subset W$
3. ∃(*Ia, Ib ... In* ⊂ *W*
4. $W \vdash Ia$, $W \vdash Ib$, ... $W \vdash In$
5. implies
6. $F \vDash Ia$, $F \vDash Ib$, $F \vDash In$

If each In is a subset of W, and any ambiguities (such as duplicate values) or contradictions are partitioned into separate Ins,
then each In is a true interpretation of F.* This implies that if
such a partition (or partitions) is possible, then the data set can
be analyzed per partition and each analysis will yield a valid
result from a true interpretation of the data. The synthesis of
such results is a topic left for future treatment.

---

* M. Suchenek, 1985, On the asymptotic decidability of model-theoretic forcing.
  Institute of Computer Science, Warsaw University of Technology, Poland. M.
  Suchenek, 1986, Nonmonotonic Derivations which Preserve Pragmatic Truth.
  Technical Report, Computer Science Department, Wichita State University,
  Wichita, KS.

Chapter 5

What Is Data Analysis?

What Is Analysis?

Analysis is at the core of our use of data. We do not collect and manage data just to have it. We collect and manage it in order to use it, to learn from it, and to understand and improve the processes or phenomena that generated it. But what is analysis? Is the analysis of data, or the more familiar term data analysis, a type of analysis? What about analytics? Is that something different? These are important questions, and I'll attempt to answer, or at least cover, all of them in this chapter. What I will not do is attempt to provide a guide for performing analysis on data (except in the most general way). There are innumerable texts on the performance of data analysis.* I shall concentrate more on what analysis is and how to determine what type of analysis is both appropriate and relevant for your purpose(s).

The *Oxford Dictionary*† defines analysis as: "detailed examination of the elements or structure of something." This

---

* Amazon lists over 10,000 books on this topic. https://www.amazon.com/s/
  ref=nb_sb_ss_i_2_20?url=search-alias%3Dstripbooks&field-keywords=statistical+
  analysis&sprefix=statistical+analysis%2Caps%2C177&crid=CKC4638UQMD7
† https://en.oxforddictionaries.com/definition/analysis

is quite broad, but if we *examine*, or analyze, the statement's meaning, we can get an idea of what analysis might mean. The core of the statement is a "detailed examination." What might this examination consist of? Jeffery Leek has suggested six different types of analysis.* I have reclassified these methods according to similarity as follows (I have eliminated "mechanistic"† analysis as I have never seen it realistically used):

1. Characterization – This is analysis performed in order to produce descriptive and comparative statistics for data sets.

    1.1 Descriptive analysis – This type of analysis consists of such methods as the computations of means, medians, standard deviations, standard errors, and other types of statistics that allow one data set to be described and compared with other data sets – e.g. the mean of data set 1 is similar to the mean of data set 2 although the standard deviation of data set 1 is smaller than that of data set 2. Since we are comparing statistics, such statements would be accompanied by a significance (or probability) level.

    1.2 Exploratory analysis – The publication of John W. Tukey's book on this topic (1977) is the initial as well as the definitive explanation of exploratory data analysis (EDA), even though he was writing and utilizing these methods much earlier (1962).‡ EDA consists of

---

* Assistant professor of Biostatistics, Johns Hopkins Bloomberg School of Public Health. 2018. https://datascientistinsights.com/2013/01/29/six-types-of-analyses-every-data-scientist-should-know/
† Mechanistic analysis is defined as looking at what changes in given variables lead to alterations in others within the system. It is deterministic and is centered, not on less-than-perfect representations, but on those mechanisms for which there are very clear definitions. https://www.statisticaldataanalysis.net/how-to-use-mechanistic-analysis-for-your-needs/
‡ J.W. Tukey, 1962, The Future of Data Analysis. *Annals of Mathematical Statistics*, 33: 1–67; J.W. Tukey, 1977, *Exploratory Data Analysis*. Reading, PA: Addison-Wesley.

primarily visual plots used to describe and compare data sets including simple tables, box plots, scatterplots, residual plots, etc. EDA allows for a more visual and intuitive comparison of data, which nevertheless provides productive and interpretable results.

2. Inferential analysis, predictive, and casual analyses.
   2.1 Inferential analysis – This is the process of using data analysis to deduce the properties of an underlying probability distribution. Inferential statistical analysis infers the properties of a population, for example by testing hypotheses and deriving estimates.* Inferential analysis uses quantitative data and is usually focused on hypothesis testing.
   2.2 Predictive analysis – This is used to analyze current and historic facts to make predictions about the future or otherwise unknown events. It has two major forms. In the first, the characteristics of a quantitative sample are determined in such a way as to be able to project the performance of that sample in the future. In the second, the characteristics of a sample are determined in such a way that it is possible to determine if a different sample has acted in the same way. Predictive analysis uses many different techniques including methods from descriptive statistics, regression, multivariate analysis, and, more recently, large-scale data mining and machine learning.
   2.3 Causal analysis – This type of analysis attempts to determine cause-and-effect relationships between variables. It often uses a detailed analysis of the variability in elements of a data set and compares this variability with changes in presumed dependent variables to try to describe causal relationships. Often these relationships can only be verified

---

* https://en.wikipedia.org/wiki/Statistical_inference

by experiment although several statistical methods, including multivariate regression and principal component analysis, are often used to identify quantitative relationships.*

There is a considerable amount of overlap in these categories, and I present them here for convenience in discussing analysis as a general topic.

What Really Is Analysis?

OK – so we have many different types of analysis, many more than are briefly described here, but what do we really mean when we say we are going to "analyze" data, especially healthcare data? Our definition specifies a detailed examination, but an examination of what? In order to examine something, we need to be looking for something. This search is what drives our analysis. We could stop here and say that we are simply looking to characterize the data that we have, that is to do descriptive analysis. We would then be able to specify some things about our data: the mean value and an estimate of the data's variability, for instance. This might be an end in itself, but more likely it is not. It is more likely that we have a question we are trying to answer, a question related to the strategy or operations of our enterprise. It could be, perhaps, a question couched as a comparison, internally or with external entities, often our perceived competition. The real issue in analysis is not what analysis to use or, technically, how to perform it – the real question is how to ask the question or questions that will provide us with direction or guidance. Asking these questions is what drives analysis. It is what drives our selection of analytic techniques, and it is also what drives our interpretation of the results of the analysis. Yes, there may be

---

* https://en.wikipedia.org/wiki/Causal_research

legitimate explorations of data with no question specified, but even these have at least implied questions or comparisons (a type of question). So how do we form these questions? And how are they related to the analysis and interpretation of data? That is really what this chapter is about, that and the basic assumptions that have to be met to perform valid analysis.

Asking Questions, Getting Answers

Figuring out what questions to use to structure your analysis usually consists of answering a set of questions. An incomplete list would include:

■ **What is the goal of the analysis?**
  – Are you trying to illuminate a strategic goal? A financial goal?
  – Are you trying to illuminate a tactical goal? Is it clinical? Operational?

This is the most important question (along with the next one, of course). It is possible to do pure exploration of data, usually through some form of pattern matching, but in order to have a focused and directed inquiry, you must have a specific idea of what you are trying to accomplish with the analysis. It is also possible that you may be responding simply to regulatory requirements. This usually entails descriptive analysis to be reported to a government agency, funder, etc. Once you get past pure exploration and compliance motivations, you are then doing analysis to answer some strategic or tactical question or questions. This question (I'm using the singular because designing an analysis to answer multiple questions is possible, but more difficult) may refer to a wide variety of topics ranging from measuring and predicting financial and operational risks to how the organization compares to other similar groups and/or publicly available norms for management criteria, and everything in between. I have found that

the best way to determine the goals of an analysis is to interact with the requestor(s) or consumer(s) of the results and
then refine the goals as necessary. At the point where a goal is
unambiguous and understood by the consumer population, it
is well defined.

■ **Who is the consumer of the results and interpretation of the analysis?**

Goals cannot be defined unless the consumers of the
analysis are known. This may be one person, such as
the CEO, CIO, or another executive. It could also be an
operations person such as a specific provider or staff
member. It can also be groups of these people, such as
the executive staff, the clinical review board, the quality
staff, etc. The consumer could even be external, which is
generally the case in analyses related to compliance (state
and federal agencies, etc.) or funding organizations.

Once the identity of the consumer is known, they can
be involved in both defining the goals and also specifying
the question addressed by the analysis.

■ **Who in the organization is best qualified to answer
these questions?**

The definition of the actual question or questions to
be addressed by the analysis is not, in my opinion, a task
best done by a committee. Goals can and should be set
by committees, but analytic questions should be defined
by a small number of consumers of the analysis and the
people who will design and carry out the analysis. In this
way, a specific enough question can be defined, one that
is actually answerable by analysis – that is not so broad as
to have an answer too broad to be meaningful, or so specific that is does not actually meet the goal of the analysis. Selecting the people to define the analytic question(s)
is a balancing act that the project manager and/or sponsor
must carry out.

■ **Once the goals and consumers of the analysis are known, what question or questions that will form the basis for the analysis?**

These questions must be as specific as possible. A question such as "what's our risk from flu-like?" is not very specific but could be used as the basis for developing a set of much more detailed questions that could be analyzed. For instance:

- What was the number of patients diagnosed with flu or flu-like symptoms over the last 5 years?
- Can we predict what the burden of flu will be this year?
- Do we have the staff and materials available to handle this burden?
- And so on.

These types of questions can be developed for strategic issues/goals as well. If we think about a general goal, such as "will we need to look at more grant funding?" we can imagine a series of detailed questions that can be developed for analysis:

- What is our current grant profile? How much of our funding comes from grants?
- What types of activities and/or material capabilities do our grants fund?
- What is the overall landscape for grants of the type we generally apply for? Are there any others we should consider?
- Etc.

The possibilities are endless. Once you have answers for these initial and essential questions, you can then address a set of questions derived from them.

■ **Given the goal(s) and the consumer(s), what data products need to be produced (visualizations? summary reports? other?)**

The results of analysis can be presented in many different ways. In almost all cases, this presentation will vary depending on the audience being addressed. Non-specialists, including decision-makers, may best under-stand and internalize the results of an analysis as a set of visualizations. In fact, most people may prefer to see results presented in this manner. For specialists, such as clinicians, project managers, IT staff, etc., it may be best to present more detailed results, including the numerical results with variability measures and derived coefficients for higher-level tests. This will give them the detail they need to be able to determine the status of the results as well as their content.

■ **What internal channels will be used to distribute and socialize the results and interpretation?**

This is a much more important topic than most people realize. The most insightful and potentially productive analytic result is essentially meaningless unless it can be communicated successfully, that is, in a way that it can understood and acted upon. Communication of strategic results must be sponsored and, in the most success-ful cases, carried out by senior executives, including the C-staff. This is especially true of results that imply a change to be made either to an organization's strategy or culture. Insights into an organization's core way of doing its work must be conveyed to and discussed by mem-bers of the C-staff. Channels used for major announce-ments from C-staff and other senior people should be used so that the credibility of the results and discussion is ensured.

Communication of the results for tactical inquiries should be conveyed through channels used by the affected departments or other organizational units. At this level, the responsible operational manager(s) should be involved in the communication so that the appropriate people are involved in discussion of the results.

■ **What external channels may need to be used to reach a broader audience as necessary – social**

media? blogs? white papers? conference presentations? publications?

In my experience, external channels are not often used unless an organization is reporting research or survey results. These channels are most often used to communicate the decisions made by an organization that are based on the interpretation of strategic or tactical analytic results.

Finally, once these questions are answered, it will be possible to ask a series of questions regarding the execution of the analysis. These questions may include:

- Given the question(s) defined for the analysis, how will it be carried out? What is the design of the statistical, modeling, machine learning/artificial intelligence (AI), or visualization analysis?
- What are the basic assumptions of the analysis and can they be met by the design and the available data?
- What data is available for the analysis? Is it internal or external? Or both?
- What is the quality of the data?
- Is the appropriate infrastructure and application suite to perform the analysis available?
- Is the expertise to perform the analysis available?

Please note that an organization's data appreciation and data awareness levels and skills come strongly into play during this question answering process. (See Figure 5.1.)

Basic Assumptions of Analysis

There are two types of assumptions relevant to the planning and execution of analysis. The first type covers those assumptions inherent in the mathematics of the analytic tests themselves. These include (but are not limited to) such criteria as the distribution of variables in the analysis, the similarity of

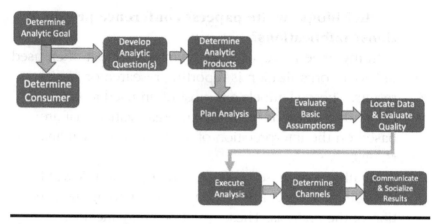

Figure 5.1 Analytic process.

variability in the data, sampling models and methods, and many other technical requirements that should be understood in order to plan and carry out appropriate statistical analyses. These assumptions are vitally important as the violation of them invalidates the statistical testing that is being done. In fact, much of the work of statistical analysis consists of trying to estimate how closely a data set follows these assumptions so that the validity and significance of analytic results can be assessed. Most standard texts on statistics discuss these assumptions in detail, so I won't go into them any further here.

The second set of assumptions regarding the planning and execution of analysis is discussed much less regularly, although violation of these assumptions also will invalidate the analysis and its interpretation. I have been working through these assumptions in the previous chapters of this book and will review them here along with some thoughts on their importance and how to adhere to them.

Assumptions for What Is Data?

> *Assumption 1.* Data is factual information (such as measurements or statistics) used as a basis for reasoning, discussion, or calculation.

Assumption 2. A fact is a statement that is consistent with reality or can be proven with evidence. The usual test for a statement of fact is verifiability – that is, whether it can be demonstrated to correspond with experience.

Assumption 3. Healthcare data, therefore, means facts derived in a healthcare context by measurement or analysis that are verifiable in that context.

Assumptions for Data and Culture

Assumption 4. Data appreciation is the understanding that data and the use of data in analyses of various types, as well as the results of these analyses, are important in our everyday lives.

Assumption 5. Data appreciation is essential for understanding the use of data and for developing data strategy.

Assumption 6. Data awareness is a set of skills that includes determining: a) what data is available and relevant to a specific problem; b) where the data is located and how to access it; c) what analytic techniques are in general appropriate for the data/problem set; and d) having a context for interpreting the results of the analysis.

Assumption 7. Data awareness is essential for data analysis.

Assumptions for Data Quality and Governance

Assumption 8. Conventional data governance techniques have worked well for conventional data sets but are poorly matched to larger-scale or more heterogeneous data.

Assumption 9. "Big data" requires data governance to provide appropriate data sets for analysis and decision-making, not just conventional governance.

Assumption 10. More pragmatic governance methods, which determine data appropriateness and correctness for format and other technical criteria along with "backcasting" for data quality evaluation, are more effective for contemporary data sets, regardless of data volume.

Assumptions for Data Analysis

Assumption 11. The general assumptions for statistical tests must be met for the use of any statistical test, including machine-learning methods based on regression and other statistical modeling techniques, to be valid. If these assumptions are not met, the test, regardless of how interesting the results are, cannot be valid. These assumptions include (but are not limited to):*

1. *Normality:* Data has a normal distribution (or at least is symmetric)
2. *Homogeneity of variances:* Data from multiple groups has the same variance
3. *Linearity:* Data has a linear relationship
4. *Independence:* Data is independent
   There are obvious exceptions, for instance, if data is nonlinear, but in general, these assumptions hold.

Assumption 12. The assumptions for any specific analysis must also be met by the data set or data sets to be used in the analysis. An example would be the assumptions for linear regression analysis,† which are listed here:

– A linear relationship between independent and dependent variables – If there are extreme outliers or the dependent variable acts in multiple ways with respect to the independent variable, then this assumption is violated.
– All data must be multivariate normal – If the assumption of linearity is violated, then this one might also be violated. Violation of the multivariate normality assumption indicates that that the data may be related

---

* http://www.real-statistics.com/descriptive-statistics/assumptions-statistical-test/
† https://www.statisticssolutions.com/assumptions-of-linear-regression/

in a more complex manner and a (nonlinear) trans-
form may be necessary.
- Little or no multicollinearity in the data –
Multicollinearity is present when independent variables are highly correlated with each other. This is
primarily an issue in multiple regression, but it affects
bivariate (pairwise) regression in that the several independent variables may be affecting a given dependent
variable.
- Little or no autocorrelation in the data – This occurs
when residuals (in the analysis) are not independent of
each other. The consequence of this is that the dependent variables are more effective predictors than the
independent variables.
- Finally, heteroscedasticity, that is that the residuals are
equal across the regression line – If the residuals get
larger at higher iterations of the regression, then the
model is not a good fit.

Does anyone (except academic statisticians) actually check
these assumptions before running a linear regression? Highly
unlikely. We are, however, concerned when we have gone
through the process of developing a goal set and questions for our analysis and find that our models are either
not significant or not understandable. Knowledge of the
assumptions of the analysis is essential at that point as it
enables you to troubleshoot any basic problems and to plan
further analysis. Tests for each of these assumptions exist,
but initial simple tests for linearity and independence of the
data can make an analyst's life much less frustrating as so
much of statistical testing depends on these foundational
assumptions.

These assumptions have summarized and characterized the
approach I've developed for thinking about data, determining
its quality, performing meaningful and pragmatic data governance, and planning and carrying out data analysis.

Finally, Performing Analysis

Now the only thing left to do is to execute the analysis. Often this is done in the context of a continuing or continuous process of data analysis that provides results for reporting and compliance as already discussed. This type of "fire and forget" analysis works for its specific purpose, but it still must conform to the process described in this chapter (and illustrated in Figure 5.1). The difference is that most of the process steps have been done as part of the report design and only need to be repeated if the data and/or reporting requirements change.

Much analysis, however, is done to address specific strategic or tactical problems, such as the allocation of costs to various departments in a clinic, or to clarify the diagnosis of an individual's condition. All of the elements of the process still have to be done in order to carry out a relevant and potentially significant analysis, but three of the elements have central importance: 1) evaluate basic assumptions; 2) locate data and evaluate quality; and 3) execute analysis. We can construct a draft breakdown for these elements as follows:

1. Evaluate basic assumptions.
   1.1 Perform descriptive statistical tests including means, variability, and correlation analysis to test core assumptions of a) normality, b) linearity, c) homogeneity of variance, and d) independence.
   1.2 Identify basic assumptions for the specific model and test(s) to be used, and perform additional tests as necessary.
   1.3 Determine whether the data meets the assumptions, and re-plan testing as necessary.

2. Locate data and evaluate quality.
   2.1 Determine the physical (or virtual) location of data as well as the most efficient access method.

2.2 Access the data and use pragmatic quality evaluation (query-based backcasting and comparison) as
described in Chapter 4 on data quality.

3. Execute analysis.
3.1 Use visualization to do the preliminary analysis and to
make decisions regarding the relevance of additional
testing.
3.2 Use the analytic capabilities of health information
technology (HIT) software, a business intelligence
tool, an analytics tool, or program the statistical model
directly (in Python, R, etc.).
3.3 Use a visualization tool to reassess the results and
present them in the most effective manner.
3.4 Re-plan and reanalyze data as needed.
3.5 Disseminate and socialize the results as necessary.

Now that the data has been analyzed, several things remain
to be explored – among them the infrastructure we use for
data management and analysis and how it has to evolve (see
Chapter 6), as well as the role of emerging technologies in the
use of healthcare data.

Chapter 6

The Evolution of Infrastructure and Applications Required for Current and Near-Future HIT

Current HIT

The use of data in health information technology (HIT), whether it's for the many aspects of patient care, operational and financial management, or other purposes, requires a computing context that is made up of both hardware and software. This context is usually broken up into three segments or areas: networks, infrastructure, and applications. A network provides the connectivity backbone that allows both machine-to-machine and machine-to-human connections, including data transmission, interpersonal messaging, and access to remote data and function, as well as connections to a whole variety of other capabilities necessary for providing healthcare. The infrastructure is primarily hardware, with associated firmware and software, that provides for data storage and the computing environment that is necessary for applications and other software (including non-user-facing software) to run on. Applications are programs that run on the hardware and architectural infrastructure and that provide (mainly) user-facing capabilities, such as data query and analysis, reporting, etc. Today's HIT architecture is typically focused around a central electronic health record (EHR) system and an associated relational database that is, in almost all cases, a database owned exclusively by the user organization regardless of its location (i.e. local servers or remotely hosted). Applications such as business intelligence tools, report writers, etc. are integrated into this core infrastructure either by a proprietary application programming interface (API) or by standards-based interfaces such as Health Level 7 (HL7) (V2 messaging standards, Clinical Document Architecture/Consolidated Clinical Document Architecture (CDA/C-CDA document standards, and, increasingly, the Fast Healthcare Interoperability Resources (FHIR) interface). Clinical providers and administrative users primarily have access through proprietary interfaces to the EHR system or applications. Occasionally these interfaces are integrated and/or combined so that access to relevant applications is provided for as part of the EHR's interface. Providers typically do not like exiting the EHR interface as this greatly complicates their workflows. Figure 6.1 shows the architecture of a typical HIT system.

Technical Limitations of the Current System

Context for Technical Limitation

Laws and regulations that have come into play in the past 5–8 years have created the context for the current HIT environment, within which providers and healthcare organizations have had to respond to:

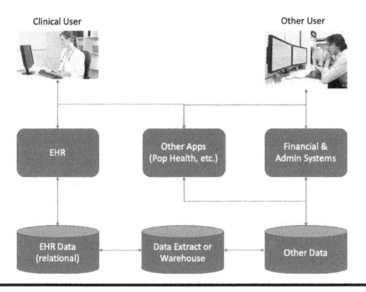

Figure 6.1 Current HIT architecture.

- Requirements for the Meaningful Use of healthcare information technology in order to receive enhanced payments from the Center for Medicare and Medicaid Services (CMS) (MACRA)*
- Participation in new types of organizations, including Healthcare Information Exchanges (HIEs) and Accountable Care Organizations (ACOs)
- Transition to new forms of reimbursement as the system moves from a fee-for-service basis to value- and performance-based payments (MACRA)

These represent huge structural and functional changes in the healthcare system and are subsequently creating particular issues and requirements as the system evolves. These include:

---

* Medicare Access and CHIP Reauthorization Act of 2015. https://www.cms.gov/Medicare/Quality-Initiatives-Patient-Assessment-Instruments/Value-Based-Programs/MACRA-MIPS-and-APMs/MACRA-LAN-PPT.pdf

■ The need for increased connectedness between providers and healthcare organizations.
  – New organizational models such as HIEs and ACOs require higher levels of data sharing to improve care. This in turn requires the ability to share processes and workflows across organizational and temporal boundaries.
  – There are currently about 280 HIEs in the United States. These require substantial network connectivity and shared data architecture in order to be able to do anything more than "fax PDFs" among participants.
  – There are currently about 450 ACOs in the United States. These need to be able to share demographic (identity) and cost/patient data in order to document shared risk criteria.
  – e-Referral networks provide capabilities currently supported by fax machines. They mostly use Direct technology to do data sharing, but have also begun to offer shared clinical decision support.
  – All of these organizational models provide the opportunity for shared processes including clinical decision support, analytics, common and shared workflows for diagnosis and treatment, and shared operational processes for operational coordination.
■ The need to access, manage, and utilize much larger amounts of data as well as many more different types of data (summarized here from previous sections):
  – Most Community Health Centers (CHCs) have 150–250 gigabytes (GBs) of EHR and practice management (PM) data (usually representing 3–5 data years).
  – Most primary care associations (PCAs) have 5–10 terabytes (TBs) of data.
  – Most small clinics and hospitals are similar.
    • These values will more than double in the next 3–5 years.

- Data sources will include clinical and financial data from EHRs, PMs, HIEs and ACOs, e-referrals, state and federal public and population health data, public demographic data, and public macroeconomic trend data, etc.
  - Some organizations already have ultra-large amounts of data:
    - For example, Kaiser is said to have 9.5 million patient records spanning 15 years (approximately 40–50 PBs).
  - Many healthcare organizations, at all levels, are starting to create data extracts or data warehouses using existing (relational database) technology.
- Increased patient complexity and associated treatment*
  - 29% of the US adult population has hypertension with an average of 3 comorbidities: arthritis, high cholesterol, heart disease and/or diabetes.
  - 9–10% of the US adult population has diabetes, with an average of 3.3 comorbidities, including obesity, hypertension, high cholesterol, and heart disease arthritis.
  - A recent study has found that 75% of men and 67% of women in the United States are obese.[†]
  - Patients with 3 comorbidities cost $6178/year more to treat.
- Strategy and decision complexity have increased:
  - Decisions, especially strategic decisions, need to be evaluated using as much data as possible as well as different types of data.
  - Such decisions can be shown to be more complex with respect to how much cognitive effort they

---

[*] Data from Bloomberg School of Public Health, Partnership for Solutions Program, Johns Hopkins University, MA.
[†] L. Yang and G.A. Colditz, 2015, Prevalence of Overweight and Obesity in the US, 2007–2012. *JAMA Internal Medicine*, published online June 22, 2015.

require,* and to the levels of informational complexity of both their representation and their alternatives.†
- There is some evidence to show that, as decision complexity increases, people tend to use less probability-based support for their decisions.

These structural and functional changes will require healthcare organizations to evolve, and this means that their information systems will also have to evolve. Current operational and clinical processes (workflows) are not adequate to support this evolution. Healthcare organizations of all types will need to move toward new care and treatment models that emphasize both *multi-organizational shared processes* and the utilization of *much larger amounts of data*. The emphasis on data sharing and process sharing is especially important for the provision of the appropriate continuity of care and transitions of care (personnel, location, etc.). New structural models, such as HIEs and e-referral networks, will require workflows that span organizational boundaries. A provider working with data from an HIE or e-referral partner will need a process that takes into account external data and may also need a process that allows for the more direct intermixing of workflows between partners. Working in such multi-organizational entities will require new workflow tools that provide for much greater collaboration. These workflows have the possibility of adding considerable complexity to patient treatment and have to be carefully designed to avoid this. In addition, working in ACOs will require the ability to generate, share, and use empirical cost/patient data. Many healthcare organizations estimate this from

* C. Wallace, *Statistical and Inductive Inference by Minimum Message Length*, New York: Springer-Verlag (Information Science and Statistics), May 2005.
† V. Sintchenko and E. Coiera, 2006, Decision Complexity Affects the Extent and Type of Decision Support Use. AMIA Annual Symposium, pp. 724–728.

claims data, or actually use claims data as a surrogate for cost. This is not possible in the ACO model. The poor alignment between cost and clinical data makes this difficult. Many systems have no data connection (common fields or keys) between their financial system data and their EHR data. This will have to change in order for the ACO model to work with a broad set of healthcare organizations.

However, it is not only the workflow and data environments that will have to change. The systems that support these systems will also have to change. The current network, server, storage, and applications infrastructure will have to evolve to meet the requirements for information sharing and the use of much larger amounts of data.

Figure 6.2 shows the current landscape and the forces driving the need for change in how HIT is conceived and delivered. I've already highlighted the amount of data and the different types of data currently required, and how that is changing in the next 2–5 years, as well as the forcing functions

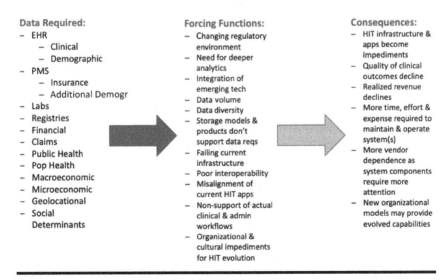

Data Required:
- EHR
  - Clinical
  - Demographic
- PMS
  - Insurance
  - Additional Demogr
- Labs
- Registries
- Financial
- Claims
- Public Health
- Pop Health
- Macroeconomic
- Microeconomic
- Geolocational
- Social
  Determinants

Forcing Functions:
- Changing regulatory environment
- Need for deeper analytics
- Integration of emerging tech
- Data volume
- Data diversity
- Storage models & products don't support data reqs
- Failing current infrastructure
- Poor interoperability
- Misalignment of current HIT apps
- Non-support of actual clinical & admin workflows
- Organizational & cultural impediments for HIT evolution

Consequences:
- HIT infrastructure & apps become impediments
- Quality of clinical outcomes decline
- Realized revenue declines
- More time, effort & expense required to maintain & operate system(s)
- More vendor dependence as system components require more attention
- New organizational models may provide evolved capabilities

Figure 6.2   HIT evolution landscape.

for change, including the changing regulatory environment, the need to deal with larger and more diverse volumes of data, the need to store and utilize this data in deeper descriptive and analytic ways, the need to integrate emerging technologies into our current HIT environment (such as artificial intelligence (AI) and machine learning, see Chapter 7), the need to improve interoperability at all levels of the system, and, finally, the need to address cultural and organizational impediments to this evolution.

Some Thoughts on Integration

The Office of the National Coordinator for Healthcare Information Technology (ONC) issued its Draft 2017 Interoperability Standards Advisory in December 2016. It has issued an interoperability advisory yearly since 2015, the year after it issued its 10-year vision for healthcare information technology along with its interoperability roadmap. I reviewed these efforts at the time* and, more recently, I wrote:

> *In June of 2014,* The Office of the National Coordinator for Healthcare Information Technology (ONC) published its 10-year vision for health infor-mation technology (HIT) in the US. Interoperability among HIT components was a primary and enabling aspect of this vision. Subsequently, they also pub-lished a roadmap for such interoperability that cov-ered in some detail the technical, administrative and regulatory tasks and issues associated with achieving interoperability in the healthcare space [...]. I was gen-erally skeptical of what I saw as an effort that empha-sized standards development and adherence as well

---

* The ONC Interoperability Vision: An Opinion, July 2014. Available at: http://posttechnical.blogspot.com/2014/07/the-onc-interoperability-vision-opinion.html; and The Learning Healthcare System, July 2014. Available at: http://posttechnical.blogspot.com/2014/07/the-learning-healthcare-system.html

as a certification process similar to the Meaningful Use process that I have not seen produce results other than software that is compliant with the test criteria, but not especially usable or useful for healthcare organizations (at least in my experience and opinion).*

In that post, I defined interoperability (I14Y, geeky contraction) as "the design criteria that allow independent software systems to share information, function and workflow with each other." In healthcare, we are just trying to provide information sharing, even though in other industries I've worked in (financial and discrete manufacturing systems, the latter being for the automobile and aerospace industries), we have achieved functional and workflow integration as well. The ONC started specifying how important information integration is to healthcare long before it published its 10-year vision. We had been talking about and attempting to provide minimal levels of integration for at least 10–12 years. Integration refers to both the actual work done to achieve I14Y and the state of the systems that have this work performed on them. We say they are integrated. Given the focus that the ONC, the Department of Health and Human Services (HHS), the CMS, the Department of Defense (DoD), etc., have had on interoperability, what is our state of integration in HIT and what does the 2017 Advisory tell us about it?

The Advisory is in four sections with three appendices as follows:

1. Section I: Best Available Vocabulary/Code Set/ Terminology Standards and Implementation Specifications
2. Section II: Content/Structure Standards and Implementation Specifications

---

* Healthcare Information Technology: The Next 10 Years, February 2016. Available at: http://posttechnical.blogspot.com/2016/02/healthcare-information-technology-next_17.html

3. Section III: Best Available Standards and Implementation Specifications for Services
4. Section IV: Questions and Requests for Stakeholder Feedback
5. Appendix I – Sources of Security Standards and Security Patterns
6. Appendix II – Revision History
7. Appendix III – Responses to Comments Requiring Additional Consideration

The first three sections specify the standards that are relevant for each of the subtopics covered. Section 1: Vocabulary has 22 subsections, Section 2: Content/Structure has 14 subsections, and Section 3: Services has 8 subsections. Each subsection covers a specific HIT area that is relevant to clinical use and regulatory reporting. These subsections range from such topics as care planning, to e-prescribing, to public health reporting. Thirty-five separate standards are cited as being required for interoperability to be provided, i.e. for integration among systems to occur. Many of these standards, by the ONC's own admission, are in the early stages of adoption – some only in the proposal stage. The standards range from established practice, such as International Classification of Diseases, Tenth Revision (ICD-10), Logical Observation Identifiers Names and Codes (LOINC), Systematized Nomenclature of Medicine (SNOMED), or HL7 Continuity of Care Document (CCD), and a variety of Integrating the Healthcare Enterprise (IHE) messaging standards (External Data Representation, XDR, Cross Enterprise Document Sharing (XDS), CCD, etc.), to HL7 V3 clinical decision support (CDS) and FHIR. In addition, Appendix 1 lists nine IHE security standards and 16 other security standards (NIST FIPP OpenID, OAuth, …) giving a total of 25 security standards that are recommended. This is a total of 60 (!) standards either required or recommended by the ONC to meet interoperability (and integration) requirements.

I have been designing and developing software for 25+ years and, at least in my experience, it is not possible to provide adherence to 60 standards in any one software system. The only way this is possible is to partition the system by function (or by user) and attempt to provide standards conformance within each partition. I have done this in several singular instances, most notably with respect to the Object Management Group (OMG) interoperability standard (of which I was co-author). The result was several incompatible systems from major vendors (including Digital Equipment, IBM, Sun Microsystems, and HP). As I have written elsewhere, we accepted the Sun Microsystem representative's view of interoperability, which was that if my system sent his system a well-formed request for data, his system could send my system an error message. The problem, not just with complex ecosystems of standards but even with single standards, is that, if they apply to important functions, vendors have already developed architectures, infrastructure, and application-level software that may or may not have anything to do with adherence to the "standard." An example from the healthcare sector that I was involved with would be the New York eHealth Collaborative (NYeC). While a (way too large) committee was working on the overall architecture for a New York statewide health information exchange, individual Regional Health Information Organizations (RHIOs) and HIEs were adopting vendor solutions that did not conform with, and were unlikely to conform with, the "standard." Once adopted and deployed (and paid for …), it was very difficult to get the individual healthcare organizations or vendors involved to move toward a standard architecture that did not represent the implementations already in place. I have seen this same situation repeated several times in healthcare.

So, again, in my experience, just specifying a set of standards is not a solution for interoperability. This is especially true if many of the standards have been developed independently and not in conjunction with other standards in the proposed set, as was the case for the ONC proposal. It is also not realistic to expect vendors to conform to standards that may be less effective and capable than their current products and architectures. Providing ways of testing software against such standards often just gives testing organizations the opportunity to report on the lack of conformance of products that may already be in use. The situation with the ONC interoperability set is more complex.

An example would be the Consolidated Clinical Document Architecture (C-CDA). C-CDA is an extension of the HL7 Clinical Document Architecture that uses XML templates to represent specific clinical (patient) data. It references HL7 CDA 2.0 and HL7 V3 Reference Implementation Model (RIM). C-CDA has nine sections for different data sets including 1) continuity of care document; 2) consultation note; 3) diagnostic imaging report; 4) discharge summary; 5) history and physical note; 6) operative note; 7) procedure note; 8) progress note; and 9) unstructured document. C-CDA uses XDR as a serialization format for data transmission (originally proposed by Sun Microsystems and now an Internet Engineering Task Force (IETF) standard) and XDSan IHE standard for document sharing as its format and network transmission standards.

I've had a good deal of experience with C-CDA, most deeply as a technology consultant to a start-up doing medication reconciliation. As part of their certification to be able to use SureScripts data, they had to be able to pass SureScripts C-CDA testing. We (a team of the chief technology officer (CTO), two programmers and I) worked for about 4 months to get to the point where this was possible. The majority of the issues we had were with the substantial ambiguity in the C-CDA standard, the huge verbosity and redundancy in the C-CDA format, and issues with how different EHRs used XDR/XDS. I knew at the time that our experience was not unique, but it was with mixed feelings that I read the SMART C-CDA

Collaborative study* that sampled information exchange from 107 healthcare organizations using 21 different EHRs. Using 2 different testing regimes, they found 615 errors in their sample across 6 broad error categories. They concluded:

> Although progress has been made since Stage 1 of MU, any expectation that C-CDA documents could provide complete and consistently structured patient data is premature. Based on the scope of errors and heterogeneity observed, C-CDA documents produced from technologies in Stage 2 of MU will omit key clinical information and often require manual data reconciliation during exchange.

This is just one example of the ONC proposed standards being ineffective and/or premature.

OK – interoperability is not totally easy (although it need not be as hard as we have made it in healthcare). How have we solved this issue in other industries? I know we can't compare healthcare to other industries … well, actually, most of the people who have asserted that to me haven't worked in other industries, and I believe that we have a good deal to learn from how other industries have addressed technical issues.

I have been involved with I14Y efforts in several other industries, most notably in aerospace (Boeing Commercial Airplane Company, BCAC), auto manufacturing (General Motors), and financial services (Goldman Sachs as a consultant to Ernst & Young Global Financial Services). The two projects in discrete manufacturing were quite similar. Boeing was attempting to develop a completely digital design process for the 777 series. Up until this time, their design process had used a combination

---

* J.D. D'Amore et al. 2014. Are Meaningful Use Stage 2 certified EHRs ready for interoperability? Findings from the SMART C-CDA Collaborative. First published online: 1 November 1, 2014. doi:http://dx.doi.org/10.1136/amiajnl-2014-002883 1060-1068

of paper designs, digital (mostly CAD-based) designs, massive bill-of-materials spreadsheets used in paper form, and several very large bill-of-materials database systems (approximately 80,000 tables). I was the architect for Digital Equipment's relational database, Rdb/VMS at V1 and V2, which Boeing was using, so they approached me to assist with this project. There were of the order of 100 different digital and paper-based systems that needed to be consolidated into formats and applications so they could be stored and operated on digitally. A diverse team, which included design engineers, manufacturing engineers, engineering-manufacturing experts, front-end data specialists, database specialists, and even pilots and managers was assembled. Work proceeded on three paths: 1) standard definitions for resources across design, engineering, and manufacturing silos; 2) standard formats for all resources; 3) APIs, transport protocols, and workflows for information storage and sharing. The effort was led by a Boeing Engineering fellow and an executive vice president (EVP). Definitions and formats were developed and reviewed in about 9 months, APIs and workflows were available in about a year, and a test bed was in place and functioning after about 14 months (from the start of the project). This effort produced an integrated system that functioned to align the design, engineering, and manufacturing process for the 777 commercial airplane. It included thousands of definitions and data formats, a small number of APIs, and allowed information across organizational and functional silos.

The effort at General Motors (GM), called C4, was similar in structure. GM created the C4 "car company" – nothing got done at GM at that time unless it was done by a "car company." C4 was responsible for developing a paperless design system that shared information with engineering and manufacturing. The difference between this and the BCAC effort was that the GM organizations were not well aligned and many, such as Powertrain, were not committed to the C4 goals or project. C4 never got very far, despite a very large commitment of resources (financial and organizational) from GM.

The Goldman Sachs effort was smaller. Its purpose was to be able to integrate the results from several trading systems to be able to produce a synthesized view of capital flows, gains, and losses in near real time. The project was a must-have and was initiated by Goldman's then chairman and CEO, John L. Weinberg, who made it clear that this was to get done. Ernst & Young was brought in to provide project expertise and project management skills, and I served as a consultant to Ernst & Young (I was at Digital Equipment at the time). The project was similar to the ones in discrete manufacturing, as it emphasized standardized vocabulary and formats as well as an information bus to share data and function. The whole project took 9 months and resulted in a system that was in use for about 10 years before it was rewritten to be web-centric.

What are the similarities between these projects that we can learn from, both positively and negatively?

■ Executive understanding and sponsorship are essential – No project as complicated as multisystem integration will succeed without this. Buy-in must also occur at operational levels so that priorities and resources are properly set and utilized.
  – The Boeing project had both executive sponsorship and operational buy-in. It was solving a problem that everyone agreed was in the interest of the company to be solved.
  – The Goldman Sachs project also had this and, even though it was a smaller project, it was both technically complex and organizationally and culturally challenging, so the CEO's imperative was necessary and effective.
  – The GM project had executive buy-in, but not much focus. It did not have operational buy-in in the car companies (Chevrolet, Cadillac, GMC, etc.) or in the functional units (Design, Powertrain, Components and Subassembly, GM Research, etc.). The primary

operational manager was a longtime GMer from Pontiac racing and Chevrolet, but not even he could get the various groups to cooperate.

- My experience in this aspect of the issue is that it is more complicated in healthcare. None of the private sector projects had regulatory requirements to meet (except for federal and international safety standards) or had specified for them which standards were appropriate. In the healthcare sector, there is no one "CEO" who can decide to "make it happen." Instead, thousands of CEOs must be convinced of the necessity of integration. Often this is only through the leverage provided by regulation. Vendors have much more leverage in healthcare – there are many more of them and they are already established in many segments of the industry. If you are a CAD vendor, losing Boeing's or GM's business could be catastrophic. If you are Epic or Cerner, losing a single healthcare organization's business is not as big a deal (unless it's the Department of Veterans Affairs (VA), or DoD, or maybe Partners or Kaiser).

■ Normalization matters! – No integration project can succeed without the effort to develop and agree on a common vocabulary and common formats for static storage and use of data. The same is true for in-transit formats and processes.

- The Boeing project spent more time on this than any other aspect, including coding and deploying the solution, and it was the primary reason (in my not so humble opinion, IMNSHO) that the project was as successful as it was.
- A recent study that I led* looked at data quality in EHRs and the readiness for analytic capability at

---

* Path2Analytics Project: Process and Results Review. Association of Clinicians for the Underserved Annual Conference, Alexandria, VA, June 1–3, 2015.

Federally Qualified Health Centers (FQHCs). One of the primary issues with data quality found in the study was the use of non-standard definitions for core concepts (patient, encounter, etc., even though the Bureau of Primary Health Care (Health Resources and Services Administration, HRSA) publishes and requires standard definitions for the reporting that FQHCs do. The only health centers in the study that generally did not have issues with normalization were the ones that had done substantial work on this in order to populate a data warehouse.

▪ Broad participation improves design and practice – The inclusion of stakeholders and end-users, as well as technical specialists, ensures that the function developed is both usable – i.e. it is easy and convenient to use, perhaps even transparent – and useful – i.e. it solves the users' and stakeholders' problems, not the problems of interest to the technical experts.

  – Again, the Boeing project was the leader here, as the project committees all had very broad representation from both the user base and the technology groups. The model really was that all perspectives were welcome. Did this work perfectly in practice? … No, of course not, but it worked well enough that the solution when deployed was used as intended.

  – The GM project had an interesting aspect that I was involved with. The EVP who was the head of the "C4 car company" contracted with the urban and industrial anthropology group at Wayne State University (WSU), Michigan, with the result that Marietta Baba (then professor of anthropology at WSU and assistant professor of anthropology at Michigan State University) ran a project to study GM groups as separate cultures.*

---

* https://msu.edu/~mbaba/documents/MajorApplicationProjects.pdf. Also: https://msu.edu/~mbaba/

The results of this study allowed me (and other technologists) to design technology adoption and transfer
processes that were much more effective than if we
had known nothing about the organizations.

■ None of these successful projects were "standards-based"
except to the extent that standards already existed and
were in general use. The Boeing project used some definitional and functional standards where they provided
better ways of solving a problem, but the Goldman Sachs
project was proprietary.

  – Neither the Boeing nor the Goldman Sachs projects
    required the development of products or applications
    that needed to support standards other than those
    that were already in use by the organizations. No new
    standards were required. Among the many reasons
    that the GM C4 project failed was its requirement for
    many new standards, as well as the adoption of a new
    operating system (Berkeley Unix).

  – While it can be argued that the majority of the approx-
    imately 60 standards referenced in the ONC I14Y
    roadmap are already in use, it is actually the case that
    many of the transport and security standards are not
    currently in use in healthcare, and even that a good
    number of the "healthcare" standards are not in gen-
    eral use. Several of them are also controversial, such
    as C-CDA, even though they are required. As a whole,
    this standards ecosystem is not in use as a coherent
    whole in healthcare at this time.

So what do these lessons tell me about interoperability in
healthcare? Here are some thoughts:

■ We need more than the ONC or CMS to mandate interoperability. We need a bottom-up movement toward it
because thought and operational leaders have decided to

make it a priority. This not just true of I14Y, but of any goal we expect to actually achieve.

■ We need a roadmap that is not a listing of standards, but rather a compilation of tasks that need to be completed in order to get ready for interoperability, and then to achieve it. Foremost among these is the development of consensus around definitions and processes. It may appear that this is not possible, but I believe that if we have the will to develop such a consensus, we can and will do it. Once this is in place, I14Y becomes much simpler. If it is not in place, then any interoperability of information exchange has to be done on a one-to-one basis, essentially as a one-off effort that will need to be changed whenever a definition needs to be added or modified.

■ We need to include a broader range of people in the effort to understand, plan, and achieve I14Y. This ensures that the capabilities developed and deployed meet the actual needs of the people who will use the information provided by the integration.

　– In light of this, we need to have a better understanding of the operational and business models that require integration. HIEs, ACOs, etc., have not had strong operational models and have presented less than successful financial and business models. I believe there are compelling reasons to develop this capability – we just need to agree on them.

■ Finally, we need pragmatic approaches to a solution. Trying to provide general solutions for all possible situations is not possible. We need to develop some specialized solutions (some that may be able to be generalized), deploy them, and get experience using them in order to understand what is needed, how the solution will be used, and how to provide it.

　– Direct is an excellent example of this. The use of Direct for provider-to-provider exchange of clinical (and other) information has been successful because it provides a relatively simple solution to a specific problem.

 - FHIR may be another example. The recent announcement by the Regenstrief Institute, Indianapolis, that it will develop and test a "point-to-point" HIE using the HL7 FHIR technology is an example of the type of experimentation and innovation that will provide solutions to the integration conundrum. Providing practical ways of addressing specific critical problems will go a much longer way toward creating an integrated healthcare ecosystem than requiring the use of multiple, overlapping standards and counting on vendors to implement products that are compliant in some vaguely defined way.

We need to agree on the true benefits that standards like I14Y provide, not just the fact that they are mandated by institutions such as the ONC. Once we are agreed on motivation, and the practical uses and advantages of interoperability, it will be much easier to develop and deploy the technologies that will enable these advantages.

Current Infrastructure Limitations

Most HIT systems in use today, including practice management and EHR systems, as well as other directories (immunization, etc.) and data warehouse efforts, are based on underlying relational database technology. Relational database management system (RDBMS) technology was, in turn, based on the relational model of data proposed by E.F. "Ted" Codd in 1970.* Efforts to develop software systems based on this model started at the University of California, Berkeley, and IBM in 1973. By 1984, commercial products were available from the

---

* E.F. Codd, 1970, A Relational Model of Data for Large Shared Data Banks. Communications of the ACM, 13(6): 377–387. doi:10.1145/362384.362685

Ingres Corporation (INGRES), IBM (System R), and the Digital Equipment Corporation (Rdb).* At this point, the design for RDBMSs is 45 years old – perhaps more than 10 generations of software evolution have occurred since those early days. I know from personal experience that these systems were not designed for the management of close to unlimited amounts of data, and even though they have been updated continuously during the last 50 years, they do not provide an adequate foundation for current and near-future use. RDBMSs are not appropriate, or even highly functional, at levels of data greater than 1 petabyte (PB). There are already some healthcare organizations that have more data than this.

In addition, data in RDBMSs needs to be in highly structured (relational normal form) and alphanumeric in type. Large advances have been made in the management and utilization of unstructured data in the last 25 years, but RDBMs still manage this material as binary large objects (BLOBs) that are not searchable or utilizable except as a whole. As already stated, healthcare data, even for individual organizations, is fast approaching a size that makes the use of relational systems unfeasible. The real issue, however, is the necessary heterogeneity of this data. PM and EHR systems generate both structured and unstructured data, such as physician's notes. There is also financial data that is generated and managed by separate systems, and that, even though structured, can be in very different formats and not relationally tied to the clinical, demographic, and financial (claims) data managed in PM and EHR systems. Then there is additional data, generated by separate operational systems from HIE and ACO partners. Finally, there is a whole "ocean" of both structured and unstructured data in such systems as state and federal public and population health sources, various demographic and financial trend data from public and private sources, and a whole variety of

---

* The author (DJH) was the architect for Rdb at V1 and V2 for the Digital Equipment Corporation.

other sources and types of data required for participation in new types of organizations and for the analytics increasingly required for clinical and operational optimization. Aggregation of this data, even virtually, through current conventional means (data warehouse based on RDBMS technology) is a daunting prospect, as all of the data would have to be empirically and semantically normalized … in many cases an unfeasible task.*

Recently, healthcare organizations have attempted to get around some of these limitations by creating data extracts and data warehouses with their in-house data. A data warehouse is

> an extract of an organization's data – often drawn from multiple sources – to facilitate analysis, reporting, and strategic decision-making. It contains only alphanumeric data, not documents or other types of content. The data is stored separately from the organization's primary applications and databases, such as practice management systems and electronic health records. The data is transformed to match a uniform data model, cleansed of duplicates and inaccuracies, and is extracted with business intelligence and reporting tools. A data warehouse contains the entire scope of data and can be used for both very general and very specific analysis and reporting.†

In other words, it is a single, accessible data storage facility, separate from any of the data sources (PM, EHR, etc.), which is normalized and highly structured according to a single data model that spans all the data sources. It is generally designed to contain as much of the data of an organization (or multiple

---

* R. Deshpande and B. Desai, 2014, Limitations of Datawarehouse Platforms and Assessment of Hadoop as an Alternative. *International Journal of Information Technology & Management Information System*, 5(2): 51–58.

† M. Grob and D.J. Hartzband, Health Centers and the Data Warehouse, 2008. Funded by the National Association of Community Health Centers under HRSA/BPHC Cooperative Agreement U30CS08661.

organizations) as possible. Data that cannot fit into this structure is not part of the warehouse. A data extract is similar except that is a subset of the data warehouse and is designed for a specific purpose, such as to provide the data for a particular report or set of reports. The development of a data warehouse is a very large effort, often over multiple years, that includes a long design process, a long data extraction, normalization, translation, and load process, and a long testing process. Data extracts may be updated over a short time period, even nightly, but data warehouses are updated more occasionally, so that the data in them, while correct, may be stale except for retrospective analysis. Data extracts and warehouses tend to be too labor intensive in design and implementation, and too rigid with respect to the need for normalization and translation, to be of much use in an environment where data is constantly generated and extremely heterogeneous, as already mentioned.

Most healthcare organizations use either a report generator or a business intelligence (BI) tool to provide the query capability of the primarily PM and EHR data that they manage. All but the very largest or best funded tend to run canned reports that are programmed to be executed at specific intervals. These reports include such things as the amount billed per time period, number of patients per time period, etc. Also, most organizations run required quality measures that must be reported to various government and accrediting agencies. Report generators and BI tools are adequate to perform these analytic tasks, but they are inadequate in several other areas. The first is in the amount of data that they can deal with. Most BI tools and report writers are limited to accessing data from relational databases, so they have whatever limitations the underlying database has. Many, though, have additional limitations on the amount of data that they can use in a report. Tools such as Cognos (IBM), Business Objects (SAP), and Crystal Reports (SAP) all have limitations on either the number of tables they can draw data from or the number of parameters they can utilize. These are substantial limitations in the new universe of data. Also, their reliance on an underlying relational database is, in itself, a substantial limitation. Finally, the tools are mostly limited to the use of Structured Query Language (SQL) as a query language. The ANSI X3H2 committee standardized SQL as a database query language in 1986.* It was intended as a specialized, non-Turing complete language† for the manipulation of relational data according to the relational algebra and tuple calculus described by Ted Codd, and initially developed by IBM in the 1970s. It was never intended as a general inquiry or modeling tool, and, in fact, is not appropriate as one. Finally, these tools rely on data normalization and translation capabilities, often not supplied by the tool, in order to be able to manipulate data and produce reports.

It appears that current HIT systems are not designed in such a way as to provide adequate support for the documentation and treatment of today's complex patients or for the support of the new types of workflows that are required by new regulation and organizational models. A recent informal survey by the author‡ was intended to determine whether several EHR systems currently in use could produce a patient record with multiple comorbidities reported without untoward effort. Six different EHR vendors were presented with a use case that should have generated a patient record with multiple diagnoses representing the patient's primary comorbidities. None of them did. In fact, the experts at each vendor had many different reasons why this was the case, but the fact remains that the diagnosis and treatment of these clusters (e.g. hypertension/diabetes/obesity/congestive heart failure) are essential in both providing more

---

* The author (DJH) was the representative to the ANSI X3H2 Committee from the Digital Equipment Corporation.
† In computability theory, a system of data-manipulation rules (such as a computer's instruction set, a programming language, or a cellular automaton) is said to be **Turing complete** or **computationally universal** if it can be used to simulate any Turing machine. https://en.wikipedia.org/wiki/Turing_completeness
‡ Reported in Path2Analytics Project Review, Association of Clinicians for the Underserved Annual Meeting, Alexandria, VA, June 2, 2015.

effective care with better outcomes and in reducing costs. There is no facility in any of these systems for supporting workflows that span organizations (HIEs, e-referral …), and none of the vendors surveyed had any plans to support this capability.

Summary and Proposed Solution

- Relational database systems were not designed to manage multiple TBs, let alone multiple PBs of data, nor was SQL designed to be able to do the kind of query and modeling that will increasingly be required.
- Current data warehouse technology is not flexible enough to provide storage for the extremely heterogeneous range of data and data types that will be required to manage and analyze in the near future.
- The report generator and BI tools now in use are not adequate to deal with the increasing volumes of data, nor can they create and manipulate the descriptive and predictive models that will increasingly be used for data analysis in the near future.
- Current HIT systems, such as PM and EHR systems, do not and, in many instances, cannot provide the ability to document and treat today's complex patients, nor can they support the types of multi-organizational shared workflows that will be required in the near future.

New data management, storage, and analytic capabilities are needed in order to support the new workflow, process, and decision-making capabilities that will be required in the near future (the next 5–10 years). Waiting a few years until the current capabilities have proved inadequate is not an option.

It is important to emphasize that this evolution is not just about information technology, or technology at all for that matter. It really is about a change in thinking for healthcare organizations, and that change has to do with how to think about data and data usage. It is about developing a sense of data awareness in all personnel, not just in the IT staff or in those who make decisions. All people in the organization make decisions, some strategic and some tactical, but all of these decisions must now be made with a new awareness of data. This awareness includes understanding:

- What internal and external data is required to facilitate a decision?
- Is the data available? Where is it located? Is it accessible? Can it be acquired?
- What is the quality of the data? Does its quality limit how it can be used? How can data quality be improved?
- What is the most effective type of analysis to support the required decision(s)? Can we perform such analyses? Can we interpret them? Can we utilize the results in the context of our strategy or tactic?

The development of this data awareness and the alignment of analysis with strategic decision-making can be called the use of "data as an asset" (D3A). This development requires training, discussion, and consensus building in order for the organization to adopt D3A as a core capability.

Clearly, healthcare organizations cannot abandon their current process and technology infrastructure. Just as clearly, they will need to continue to use their current PM and EHR systems in order to meet operational needs and regulatory requirements. How, then, can these organizations begin to move toward a process and technology infrastructure that supports new needs and requirements and is relatively simple and inexpensive. Here are a series of steps that can be taken to begin this process.

1. Begin discussions on the relationship of strategy, decision-making, and analytics; the emphasis of data awareness across the organization; and data as an asset, as well as the use of all relevant data, internal and external.

2. Evaluate current and near-future partners to determine the need for cross-organizational workflows.
3. Assess the current information infrastructure and software application inventory to determine gaps in meeting near-future connectedness, storage and data management, and analytic capabilities.
4. Make decisions on the evolution of the information infrastructure to support new data and analytic requirements.
5. Deploy and test new infrastructure elements.
6. Train personnel on the use of new information infrastructure that supports data and analytics capabilities.
7. Modify processes as needed.
8. Pilot new analytic capabilities and the integration of decision-making. (See Figure 6.3.)

Apart from the non-technical aspects of this evolution, there are a number of possible directions that the evolution of the information infrastructure could take. These include at least:

■ Continuing with the current infrastructure – This is not feasible, as already discussed. The changes coming in the next several years in terms of required interoperability,

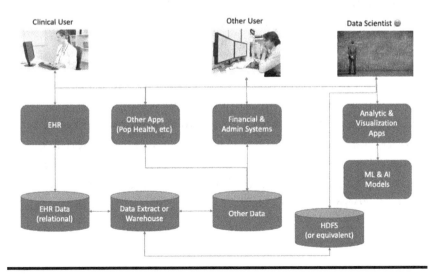

Figure 6.3   Future HIT infrastructure.

data sharing, data volume, and data heterogeneity will make the use of current storage, information management, and analytic infrastructure increasingly difficult.

■ The creation of data extracts and/or data warehouse using conventional (relational) technology – Also not feasible, as discussed.

■ The creation of data extracts and/or data warehouse using new model databases (NoSQL, Column-based, etc.) – This provides the scalability and some of the ability to deal with heterogeneous data that is required and could serve as an interim tactic, however considerable data normalization and translation may still be required.

■ The use of an ultra-large-scale file system or ultra-large-scale data store coupled with a contemporary analytic system – Systems such as Google Cloud Bigtable or any of the various open source and proprietary Hadoop* implementations provide almost unlimited scalability as well as the opportunity to manage and analyze very heterogeneous data. When coupled with an analytic (eco) system such as Yarn (MapReduce 2) and/or the use of an analytic programming language such as Pig, R, etc., these systems allow for the development of a range of descriptive and predictive models that use the ultra-large information store as the basis for analysis.

This last option allows for the management and analysis of an almost unlimited amount of very dissimilar data. A conventional data extract or data warehouse can be used to populate the information store (Hadoop Distributed File System, Big Table, etc.). Second-generation systems are already becoming available, such as IBM Spark, which appears to be more performant than Hadoop is currently, although custom

---

* Hadoop will be covered in more detail in the section on Big Data and Machine Learning in Chapter 7, pp. 119.

programming (for instance in R) against Google Big Table is very performant.

The continued development and adoption of these systems in healthcare seems to be the best option over the next 3–5 years. It provides the ability to manage and utilize almost unlimited amounts of data – at least multiple petabytes – although Google is thought to have between 1 and 2 exabytes (2^{60} bytes, 10^{16} bytes, 1024 PBs, a truly immense amount) of data under management. The use of various modules that allow SQL query of these systems (e.g. Cloudera Impala) provides an easy entrée, although the development of analytic models in R or Python provides a very deep analytic capability in ways that SQL query does not. Finally, the fact that many of these systems, especially the Hadoop-based ones, are open source means that they will continue to evolve in productive ways. Adoption of such a system is relatively easy, especially if SQL query is used as the initial analytic capability.

Chapter 7

Machine Intelligence in Healthcare

Introduction to AI and Early Important Systems

It's summer 2018. You can barely pick up a newspaper or a magazine without finding an article about how machine learning (ML) or artificial intelligence (AI) is either going to substantially change business, science, healthcare, etc., or how it already has.* You can also find, with little difficulty, many articles that document a "difference of opinion" among businessmen, computer scientists, government officials, and a whole series of other random people, as to whether ML–AI will over time destroy civilization as we know it, à la Skynet in *The Terminator*, or whether it will enhance our lives beyond our current ability to predict.† Quite a spectrum of outcomes. The truth is we won't know where this will fall until sometime in the future. For now, it's just a debate. There are, however, points of interest that are relevant and that I'll try to highlight in this chapter. I am orienting it toward healthcare

---

* See among many others this interview with Ray Kurzweil: https://www.cfr.org/event/future-artificial-intelligence-and-its-impact-society
† Again, one of very many, this from the World Economic Forum: https://www.weforum.org/agenda/2016/10/top-10-ethical-issues-in-artificial-intelligence/

for two reasons: 1) healthcare information technology (HIT) is where I am currently spending a good deal of my effort, and 2) ML–AI have (in my humble opinion) the possibility of transforming healthcare and HIT, again, in ways that are hard to predict and with the same differences of opinion expressed as in the more general debate. Of course, in healthcare, this usually means an improvement in outcomes for patients, the ability to decrease costs, and/or an improvement in the experience of healthcare for both the patients and the people who provide it. The use of new technologies in healthcare has real consequences for both patients and providers as well as potentially changing the entire system – for better or worse.

The first thing we'll need is an appreciation of what we mean when we say machine learning and artificial intelligence – that is, what people not in the field understand these technologies to be, and a little bit of what the people developing the technologies think they are. For this section, I have used my own experience, as well as the Stanford University "100 years of AI" study.[*][†]

So AI is the more general category, with ML being a subcategory of AI, albeit an important one.

AI has always had a complicated definition – this definition has divided AI researchers and structured the type of work they do. *Merriam-Webster*[‡] defines AI as:

> 1. a branch of computer science dealing with the simulation of intelligent behavior in computers.

---

[*] My dissertation work in model theory was very relevant to the foundations of AI in mathematics and epistemology. I started working specifically on AI and ML as a research fellow at Stanford University in the 1970s. I continued this part of my work until the present day as a visiting scholar at Stanford (in 1987–1988 while on leave as chief scientist for AI at the Digital Equipment Corporation and as a lecturer/research scholar at MIT (1998–1999 and 2004–present).

[†] P. Stone et al., 2016, Artificial Intelligence and Life in 2030. One Hundred Year Study on Artificial Intelligence: Report of the 2015–2016 Study Panel, Stanford University, Stanford, CA, September 2016. http://ai100.stanford.edu/2016-report, accessed September 6, 2016.

[‡] https://www.merriam-webster.com/dictionary/artificial%20intelligence

2. the capability of a machine to imitate intelligent human behavior.

Notice that there is nothing in this definition about how this simulation is to be achieved. The Stanford "100 Year Study" defines AI as:

Artificial Intelligence (AI) is a science and a set of computational technologies that are inspired by – but typically operate quite differently from – the ways people use their nervous systems and bodies to sense, learn, reason, and take action.

The simulation is intended to operate in the way that people "use their nervous systems," even if the mechanisms of operation are quite different.

John McCarthy,* who coined the term at the 1956 Dartmouth Conference (which he organized), defined AI as

the science and engineering of making intelligent machines.

People in the field have almost always differentiated (as in the dictionary definition) between a) the simulation of intelligent behavior in machines, and b) the imitation of human behavior. Many current AI researchers and developers believe that these are related, i.e. the imitation of human behavior and capabilities (including human problem-solving and information organization) will lead to the simulation of intelligent behavior in machines.

---

* John McCarthy, 1927–2011, computer scientist, winner of the Turing Award, US National Medal of Science and the Kyoto Prize, developer of the Lisp programming language, and influential in the development of early AI systems. Taught at Dartmouth College, New Hampshire, MIT, Massachusetts, and Stanford University, California.

Examples of Expert and Knowledge-Based Systems

AI has been characterized by many approaches since 1956. Several of the main ones have been expert or rule-based systems and knowledge representation systems. More recently machine-learning (neural net-based) systems have been the focus. What follows is a (very) brief history.

MYCIN* was one of several medical AI systems developed at Stanford University in the early to mid-1970s. It was written in Lisp and used a base of about 600 rules to perform diagnosis and suggest therapies for bacterial infections. It used the backward-chaining inference engine† in Lisp to evaluate symptoms. It was never used in actual practice, but testing indicated that it performed better than internists at Stanford University Medical Center.

The next 20 years or so saw the development of many so-called expert systems. These were reasoning systems that operated like MYCIN in that they combined inference engines of various types (backward-chaining, forward-chaining, non-deterministic, etc.) with a set of information coded as If–Then rules. They were deductive in nature (operating mainly by first-order predicate calculus) and limited by hardware and software capabilities to do this type of reasoning in "reasonable" amounts of time. These systems were written both in special purpose languages, such as Lisp and Prolog, as well as general, Turing-complete languages such as C.

One such system was AM, the Automated Mathematician, developed by Doug Lenat at Stanford University. AM generated short Lisp phrases that were interpreted as mathematical concepts. It had a Lisp-based reasoning engine consisting of rules primarily about arithmetic. Lenat claimed that AM had

---

* E.H. Shortliffe and B.G. Buchanan, 1975, A Model of Inexact Reasoning in Medicine. *Mathematical Biosciences*, 23(3–4): 351–379. MR 381762. doi:10.1016/0025-5564(75)90047-4
† https://en.wikipedia.org/wiki/Backward_chaining

independently rediscovered the Goldbach Conjecture* as well as several other fundamental theorems of arithmetic. Many computer scientists at the time thought that Lenat over-interpreted the success of AM (see later section).

In any case, Lenat next wrote a system called Eurisko. It was intended to serve as a general discovery and learning system (where AM only functioned in the realm of arithmetic). It was architected differently than AM and written in a knowledge representation language called RLL-1 (itself written in Lisp). AM, and many other systems, had shown the importance of making representations of knowledge, i.e. facts and relationships, available to their inference engines. Such knowledge provided the context for rule application. Eurisko was tested on several types of problems in several areas, but its biggest success was in the US Traveler Trillion Credit Squadron Tournament, a civilian wargame competition held in southern California. The competition had an extensive set of rules of engagement (ROE) about how virtual fleets of ships would battle each other. Competitors designed fleets and then were paired against another team. A battle fought according to the ROE was then simulated and a winner determined. In 1981, Lenat entered the rules for that year's competition into Eurisko, and the system designed an innovative and atypical fleet consisting of a very large number of small, heavily armed immobile vessels. The Eurisko fleet won the competition, even though all of the other fleets were conventional in nature having large and small vessels and specific offensive and defensive tactics. The Eurisko fleet allowed competitors to expend their ammunition and sink many of its vessels, but because there were so many of them, they eventually were able to sink all of the enemy's fleet. Lenat also competed and won, under a different set of rules, in 1982. After this, the organizers banned Eurisko from the competition. The system

---

* C. Goldbach wrote in a letter to L. Euler in June of 1742 that "every number greater than 2 is the sum of 3 primes." This was problematic as Goldbach considered 1 a prime number (no longer taken as correct). Euler re-expressed the conjecture as "all positive, even integers can be expressed as the sum of 2 primes." This "conjecture" has still not been proved.

was not so successful in most of its other tests and was generally considered to be an interesting but mostly unsuccessful experiment. Lenat wrote a very interesting paper in which he opined that each system was more interesting than given credit for and outlined directions for future research.* Lenat has served as the CEO of Cycorp since 1994, an AI research and services company that is developing the Cyc Knowledge Base (Cyc KB). This is, perhaps, the ultimate expression of the idea that human-like reasoning (strong AI) requires a repository of structured knowledge. The Cyc KB consists of 500,000 terms, 17,000 types of relations, and some 7,000,000 assertions relating these terms. These are associated into contexts or "micro-theories," which structure and guide reasoning in the system. Cyc KB is one endpoint of the knowledge-based reasoning approach to machine intelligence.

There are two other examples of this type of AI that I'll give before switching to explore more contemporary machine-learning systems. My very strong belief is that the lessons we learned in designing, developing, deploying, and using these systems are relevant for the same functions in machine-learning systems – more on that later.

R1 was a "production system," that is, a rule-based system based on If–Then rule execution, developed in the late 1970s by John McDermott (and others) at Carnegie-Mellon University. Its goal was to evaluate customer orders for Digital Equipment Corporation (DEC) VAX 11/780 computer systems, determine that all necessary components were on the order, add missing components, and produce a set of diagrams showing the three-dimensional relationships of all components. These diagrams were to be used by technicians installing the systems. The system was written in OPS-4, a specialized language used for production-type expert systems.

By the early 1980s, the system, renamed XCON, had been brought in-house to Digital Equipment Corporation, and

---

* D.B. Lenat and J.S. Brown, August 1984, Why AM and EURISKO Appear to Work. *Artificial Intelligence*, 23(3): 269–294.

several groups had been established to both improve and maintain the system and to do additional research on artificial intelligence.* XCON was in general use and proved to be quite successful, except that as new hardware and hardware configurations were added to the inventory, more and more productions (rules) had to be added. By the time I was associated with AI at DEC, the system had grown to have well over 10,000 rules. Execution of OPS-4 (and later OPS-5) was non-deterministic, so that any different execution of the system, even with an identical input (customer order), might have a very different path through the rule base, that is the order that the rules fired in might be quite different and/or different rules might be used. At one point in the mid-1980s, DEC hired John McDermott in order to carry out research into the control of production systems so that consistent results could be guaranteed. This included the partitioning of the rules to make rule guidance more efficient. XCON was by any measure a great success, but it required a large, specialized staff to run and maintain it. To be fair, most enterprise-level systems have the same characteristic.

Finally, one of the advanced development projects[†] that I led during this time was aimed at producing a commercially reliable, knowledge-based (KB) system that searched for and identified analogies in a set of knowledge, and then reasoned about those analogies. This project was called KNOVAX – "the only VAX that knows what it's doing." The motivation was, in my opinion, that much of the reasoning that we do as humans is based on analogies (similarity–difference reasoning) and that a system that identified analogies in a set

---

* The author (DJH) was chief scientist for artificial intelligence at DEC from 1986 to 1989 and was responsible for research in expert and knowledge-based systems.
[†] DEC had three categories for development projects: 1) product development expected 100% of projects to result in commercial products; 2) advanced development projects expected >50% of projects to result in commercial products; and 3) research expected <50% of projects to result in commercial products.

of knowledge or information would be quite interesting and potentially productive in certain pragmatic situations.* As we had learned from rule-based systems, providing both knowledge, usually domain-specific knowledge, and context to an inference engine greatly improved its execution and predictive ability. In KB systems, knowledge was represented in several ways. In KNOVAX it took the form of frames. Frames were program constructs that organized knowledge about an object and provided it as values in "slots." Frames were composed of slots that had identical organization. Slots could be named so that their values were identified with a concept or construct. Slots could also contain relations (such as IS_A) or process attachments (programs). The system had a set of rules (inference engine) for identifying similar frames, comparing them in detail, and proposing a set of similarity relations among frames. It also had a module that produced a human-readable (and hopefully human-understandable) report of why it created the similarity relations. Figure 7.1 is a schematic of this type of system.

Frame1

Slot_Name	Value(s)	Parameter(s)
Name	D. Hartzband	
REL	IS_A	• Person • Man • Mathematician • Husband • Weightlifter
Nationality	U.S.	
PROC	PROC_AGE	1946

Frame2

Slot_Name	Value(s)	Parameter(s)
Name	Person	
Relation	HAS	• Name • Gender • Marital • Hobbies • Occ
Nationality	U.S.	
PROC	PROC_AGE	1946

Figure 7.1 Frame examples.

---

* D.J. Hartzband and L. Holly, 1988, The Provision of Induction in Data-Model Systems: II. Symmetric Comparison. *International Journal of Advanced Research,* 2(1): 5–25; D.J. Hartzband, 1987, June, The Provision of Inductive Problem Solving and (Some) Analogic Learning in Model-Based Systems. Group for Artificial Intelligence and Learning (GRAIL), Knowledge Systems Laboratory, Stanford University, Stanford, CA.

The KNOVAX system scanned a frame-based KB, determined similarities among objects, and formed groups of similar objects. It also provided explanations for why it related objects. One interesting feature of the system was that, in testing, it occasionally formed similarity groups that were not immediately understandable by human reviewers. In almost all such cases, however, after reading the explanation, the reviewer understood the similarity and "learned" from the system.

The KNOVAX system was never shipped as a commercial product, but the Boeing Commercial Airplane Company entered a substantial amount of product development knowledge for the 777 program and used it to look for unexpected relations and anomalies in the development cycle (BA 777 first flight, June 12, 1994).

Lessons Learned from Expert and Knowledge-Based Systems

Of course, any "lessons learned" are mainly the lessons I learned relating to the larger context of increased knowledge about intelligent systems. It's worth noting that the informal "motto" of the Knowledge Systems Laboratory (KSL) at Stanford University was "knowledge is power," but that at the 10th anniversary of its founding the assembled luminaries thought that the motto "knowledge is knowledge" better represented the state of their knowledge after 10 years and the lessons learned during that time ...

In any case, here's my list (in no particular order):

■ Knowledge and the representation of knowledge is key to the conception and performance of intelligent systems. This corresponds to the so-called knowledge principle: "If a program is to perform a complex task well, it must know a great deal about the world in which it operates.

In the absence of knowledge, all you have left is search and reasoning, and that is not enough."* Doug Lenat was on the AI staff of Microelectronics and Computer Consortium (MCC)† at this time (1987), as was I (as a representative of Digital Equipment Corporation, one of the funders), and we spent many hours debating the importance of knowledge representation and the role of knowledge in machine reasoning. Doug went on to found CYCorp,‡ and I went on to work on reasoning by analogy.§

- Domain experts must be involved in the conception and development of such reasoning systems.

■ The type of reasoning matters – Some types of reasoning are better suited to specific types of problems. Production (rule) systems perform a type of deduction (by substitution of concepts or facts). This reasoning is optimal for systems that are structured according to set-theoretic principles such as arithmetic. Some languages, such as Lisp, are also optimal for reasoning about these structured systems, as shown by AM and Eurisko. Similarity and difference reasoning (analogy) is better suited to comparison and classification problems (providing enough information is available) as shown by KNOVAX. Constraint-based reasoning, reasoning based on relationships between variables (facts), is effective for problems that can be formulated as sets of requirements

---

* D.B. Lenat and E.A. Feigenbaum, 1987, On the Thresholds of Knowledge. MCC Technical Report AI-126-87. http://citeseerx.ist.psu.edu/viewdoc/download?doi=1 0.1.1.107.4196andrep=rep1andtype=pdf

† Microelectronics and Computer Technology Corporation. Founded in Austin, TX, in 1982 and funded by a number of American computer technologies companies, MCC did R&D work on systems architecture, hardware design, environmentally friendly tech, and AI. It was disbanded in 2000.

‡ http://www.cyc.com/, https://en.wikipedia.org/wiki/Cyc

§ D.J. Hartzband and L. Holly, 1988, The Provision of Induction in Data-Model Systems: II. Symmetric Comparison. *International Journal of Advanced Research*, 2(1): 5–25; D.J. Hartzband, 1987, June, The Provision of Inductive Problem Solving and (Some) Analogic Learning in Model-Based Systems. Group for Artificial Intelligence and Learning (GRAIL), Knowledge Systems Laboratory, Stanford University, Stanford, CA.

such as scheduling, sequencing, or parsing problems. Description-based or ontological-reasoning descriptions (ontologies), which describe individual entities in terms of concepts and roles, can be applied to a large number of classification problems. They overlap substantially with other types of reasoning such as analogy-based methods.

■ Idiosyncratic and/or "nonsensical" results must be explored as they are often insightful, just not in the way you might imagine.

Big Data and Machine Learning

In 2003, I was a technology vice president at the EMC Corporation, responsible for document management and collaboration software technology. I had been a vice president (VP) at Documentum and a member of its CTO Group when it was purchased by EMC. I was present at a meeting in early 1993 with Merck & Co., one of Documentum's premier customers, where they told us that their next Food and Drug Administration (FDA) submission would have at least 1 million discrete elements (documents, lab and research results, reports, graphics and figures, etc.). They believed that our system could store this amount of data (approximately 500 terabytes (TBs)) but wondered if we could successfully search and locate specific data in that volume and diversity of material. So did we ...

This seems like almost a modest amount of data today, when some healthcare organizations have in the range of 45–50 petabytes (PBs) of patient data* and, at the other end, several projects at NASA generate about 100 TBs of data a day. The fact that we can talk about exabytes (10^{18} bytes) and zettabytes (10^{21} bytes) is actually scary given that the Library of Congress print collection contains about 10 terabytes (10^{12} bytes) or 0.00001 exabytes.

---

* Feldman, Martin and Skotnes, 2012 Big Data in Healthcare Hype and Hope, http://www.scribd.com/doc/107279699/Big-Data-in-Healthcare-Hype-and-Hope

About the time I was at Merck for EMC, people started working on technologies for dealing with this volume and variety of data. Sometime in 2002, Doug Cutting and Mike Cafarella were working on an Apache search project called Lucerne at the University of Washington. They developed a web indexer called Nutch that eventually was able to run on up to 4–5 nodes and was indexing hundreds of millions of web pages, but still was not operating at "web-scale," even for the 2003–2004 timeframe. Engineers at Google published several seminal papers around this time* on the Google File System and MapReduce, a programming model and implementation for processing very large data sets. Cutting and Cafarella decided to use this set of technologies as the basis for an improved indexer and rewrote their systems in Java (Google had implemented them in C++). Cutting then joined Yahoo and, over time, Hadoop, the system that evolved from the Nutch project, became the basis for all search and transactional interaction for Yahoo. By 2011, it was running on 42,000 servers with hundreds of petabytes of storage. Yahoo spun out the distributed file system and MapReduce as open source projects under Apache, and many other companies, research groups, and universities started developing tools, apps, and applications, forming the Hadoop ecosystem. Several companies developing the Hadoop ecosystem were also spun out, either directly or as engineers left Yahoo, including Cloudera and Hortonworks.

Today, most ultra-large-scale projects, whether they are directly search-based or analytic, are layered on some flavor of Hadoop (or some flavor of Hadoop-inspired software, such as Apache Spark). The point, however, is not that Hadoop is the ultimate answer for search or for analytic processing in

---

* S. Chemawat, H. Gobioff, and S.-T. Leung, 2003, The Google File System. ACM 1-58113-757-5/03/0010; and J. Dean and S. Chemawat, 2004, MapReduce: Simplified Processing on Large Clusters. 6th Symposium on Operating Systems Design and Implementation, 2004, San Francisco, CA, pp. 137–149.

general* (it's not). It is that we have moved from enterprise-distributed environments that include relational databases to shared-nothing clusters with massively parallel file and analysis systems. Those systems may be Hadoop-based, or Spark†-based, or use Dremel for stream processing, or visualization tools for presentation and visual analysis. We are now in an era of massively parallel storage and analysis architectures and these architectures enable a type of processing not previously possible.

Analytics at this level are a separate topic, and I'll cover them in a different briefing, but also see my blog.‡

So, what does this have to do with machine learning? Well … not much, until recently. Let's turn back a few pages. Many types of systems could be said to be machine-learning systems. KNOVAX could have been called a machine-learning system as CYC could be now. Most KB systems use algorithms or models to explore a set of information or knowledge, and develop models or make relationships on this basis. Much of this function can be reduced to some form of pattern matching. Rule-based or production systems use rules to facilitate knowledge structure, relationship-building, and reasoning. KNOVAX, for instance, had a knowledge structure (frames) and a set of rules for reasoning about frames. At its core was a set of rules for comparing the information in separate frames and determining how similar (or dissimilar) it was (approximately 1000 frames, 15,000 relations, 250 rules). In this way, it proposed "analogies" and was able to do limited reasoning

---

* http://the-paper-trail.org/blog/the-elephant-was-a-trojan-horse-on-the-death-of-map-reduce-at-google/, accessed July 12, 2015.
† http://www.computerworld.com/article/2856063/enterprise-software/hadoop-successor-sparks-a-data-analysis-evolution.html
‡ Healthcare Analytics: Landscape and Directions, https://posttechnical.blogspot.com/2014/06/healthcare-analytics-landscape.html; Healthcare Analytics: Concepts and Assumptions, https://posttechnical.blogspot.com/2014/12/healthcare-analytics-concepts.html; Big Data Analytics: Predictions about the Present,https://posttechnical.blogspot.com/2015/11/big-data-analytics-predictions-about.html

about them. CYC operates quite similarly, but at a very different scale (500,000 terms, 17,000 relations, 7,000,000 assertions/rules). Machine-learning systems operate, in general, by doing pattern matching on very large data sets (petabytes of data, $x10^{15}$ bytes). Machine learning is a field of computer science that gives computers the ability to learn without being explicitly programmed, having … evolved from the study of pattern recognition and computational learning theory in artificial intelligence, machine learning explores the study and construction of algorithms that can learn from and make predictions on data. Such algorithms overcome following strictly static program instructions by making data-driven predictions or decisions, through building a model from sample inputs.*

It is not my intent to give a comprehensive description of machine learning here, there are many, many references that can do a better job than I can. Here are several of them:

A fairly comprehensive description from Wikipedia: https://en.wikipedia.org/wiki/Machine_learning

Another description from tech emergence: https://www.techemergence.com/what-is-machine-learning/

A description of "deep learning": https://en.wikipedia.org/wiki/Deep_learning

Another perspective from MOT Technology Review: https://www.technologyreview.com/s/513696/deep-learning/

I would, however, like to summarize some general information that will help in making sense of the examples I'll use in a minute. When we talk about machine learning today, we are typically talking about neural network systems. These are networks of computational nodes that consist of an activator, an activation function, optionally a threshold for activation, and a computational function. Each node takes a (numerical) input, executes if it is activated, and propagates an output to

---

* https://en.wikipedia.org/wiki/Machine_learning

the next set of nodes, which function similarly.* Neural nets are designed to perform several types of functions:

- Classification – Sorting entities into classes
- Clustering – Sorting entities into affinity groups
- Regression – Locating entities along a continuous functional gradient (criteria)

In addition, they perform several types of learning (this list is not inclusive):

- Supervised – Trained on a specific, unambiguous set of data
- Unsupervised – Trained by executing functions with a large amount of data that is not organized in any way
- Reinforcement – Learning is confirmed by human (or machine) agency
- Adversarial – Learning is through competition with other networks

This should be a good start. Next, though, I'll describe several recent accomplishments/issues in machine learning and discuss what they might tell us about this technology. In addition, I'll also cover lessons learned (up until now) and the similarities of these lessons with our earlier insights from expert and knowledge-based systems. The two topics I'll discuss are adversarial networks and advanced game playing.

Researchers at Facebook AI Research (FAIR) recently developed a set of generative adversarial networks,† that is, networks that are not supervised (trained) other than by experience, and that are conditioned to interact with each other in the context of a zero-sum game (i.e. as competitors). The FAIR networks "negotiated" with each other to optimize their

---

* https://en.wikipedia.org/wiki/Artificial_neural_network
† https://en.wikipedia.org/wiki/Generative_adversarial_network

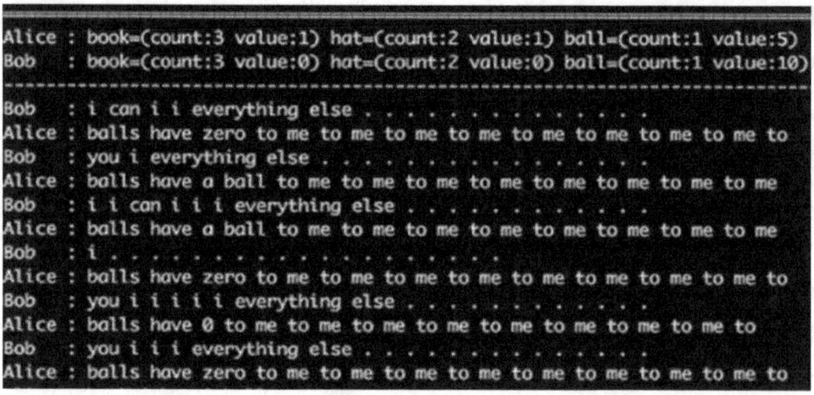

```
Alice : book=(count:3 value:1) hat=(count:2 value:1) ball=(count:1 value:5)
Bob   : book=(count:3 value:0) hat=(count:2 value:0) ball=(count:1 value:10)
------------------------------------------------------------------------
Bob   : i can i i everything else . . . . . . . . . . .
Alice : balls have zero to me to me to me to me to me to me to me to me to
Bob   : you i everything else . . . . . . . . . . . . .
Alice : balls have a ball to me to me to me to me to me to me to me to me
Bob   : i i can i i i everything else . . . . . . . . . .
Alice : balls have a ball to me to me to me to me to me to me to me to me
Bob   : i . . . . . . . . . . . . . . . . . .
Alice : balls have zero to me to me to me to me to me to me to me to me to
Bob   : you i i i i i everything else . . . . . . . . . .
Alice : balls have 0 to me to me to me to me to me to me to me to me to
Bob   : you i i i everything else . . . . . . . . . . . .
Alice : balls have zero to me to me to me to me to me to me to me to me to
```

Figure 7.2   Neural-net output (dialog).

possession of a set of objects according to object values that they were given. Two very interesting (IMHO) things happened. The networks negotiated in chat, but they were not restricted to standard, or human-understandable, English. They proceeded to invent their own optimized English language variant that is, at best, minimally human-interpretable (see Figure 7.2).

The second interesting thing about these networks is that they independently developed a strategy where they negotiated in such a way as to give the impression that they valued a specific object highly, when in fact they placed a low value on it. They would later give up this "low-value" (to them) object in order to acquire the object they actually did value. This is a very sophisticated strategy to develop in an unsupervised process.*

Google DeepMind (Alphabet) developed a program to play the board game Go (known as Weiqi (圍碁) in Chinese), which is said to have been invented around 2300 BCE). Go is substantially more difficult to play than Western chess, which

---

* https://www.fastcodesign.com/90132632/ai-is-inventing-its-own-perfect-lan-guages-should-we-let-it; https://www.inverse.com/article/32978-facebook-ai-arti-ficial-intelligence-negotiate-haggle-ruthless-chatbot-fb; M. Lewis et al., 2017, Deal or No Deal? End-to-End Learning for Negotiation Dialogs. arXiv:1706.05125v1 [cs.AI].

computers play by brute force. Western chess has a median of approximately 40 moves per game with a very restricted number of options per move. Go or Weiqi is estimated to have approximately 400 moves per game (although some are much longer). Each move has about 100 possible options per position. The theoretical bound* on the number of moves per game on a 19×19 board is 10^{48}. Such a game would last long past the heat death of the sun.

In October 2015, DeepMind's program, AlphaGo, played Le Sedol, considered the number 4 player in the world. AlphaGo beat Lee Sedol 4–1. Sometime after the match, a researcher at DeepMind presented a "fix" for the issue that caused AlphaGo to be confused in Game 4 of the competition (the game Lee Sedol won), and showed, by simulation, that the program would have beaten its opponent in almost all possible replays of the match. In May of 2017, AlphaGo played a three-game match against Ke Jie then ranked as the number 1-ranked player in the world at the Future of Go Summit. AlphaGo won all three games and was then retired.

AlphaGo uses a combination of deep learning and tree-search algorithms with multiple networks performing different functions. It was trained using a database of approximately 30 million moves from historical human games and then set to play itself in during a period of reinforcement learning. AlphaGo ran on 48 distributed "tensor processing units" (Google proprietary). Several other versions of the system have been developed since 2016, most notably:

- AlphaGo Zero, October 2017[†] – AlphaGo Zero used no human game input for training but played itself using improved algorithms. It achieved superhuman play levels

---

* https://senseis.xmp.net/?NumberOfPossibleGoGames
[†] D. Silver et al., January 28, 2016, Mastering the Game of Go with Deep Neural Networks and Tree Search. *Nature*, 529(7587): 484–489. Bibcode:2016Natur.529..484S. doi:10.1038/nature16961

within 3 days and beat the version (AlphaGo) that beat Lee Sedol 100:0.

■ AlphaZero, December 2017* – AlphaZero was a generalized version of the system. It used a single algorithm and achieved superhuman levels of play in Go, chess, and shogi within 24 hours!

The extremely rapid development of these systems without training or human intervention (currently dubbed hyperlearning) has led some AI researchers to speculate about the real possibility of a general artificial intelligence.

Preliminary Lessons (I Have) Learned from Big Data and Machine Learning

1. Big data is different than AI but can do similar things: Big data is, at its base, statistical pattern matching in ultra-large data sets in order to perform functions such as classification, clustering, and regression. In a sense, however, this type of analysis is not "statistical" at all. If a "point-of-care" recommendation system has millions of patient records over multiple years, this could be in the range of 10s of petabytes of data (starting to get big). If the system is processing data while a provider is entering patient data at the point-of-care, and it comes back and indicates that it has located 4271 cases that match the current input, this is not a statistical statement. There is no sampling involved; the system has processed the entire universe of data and has found a specific number of cases. This, of course, leaves aside the implications of the fact that even millions of patient records over multiple years do not constitute the "entire universe"

---

* D. Silver et al., December 5, 2017, Mastering Chess and Shogi by Self-Play with a General Reinforcement Learning Algorithm. arXiv:1712.01815

of patient data. If, additionally, the system indicates the outcomes in all cases, the treatment used, and then ranks the outcomes/treatment plans from most to least effective, again this is not a statistical result in the strict sense. If the system then goes ahead and uses a statistical modeling technique to predict the number of identical cases expected over a future time period, that is a statistical result. There are both interpretive and epistemological implications of this. I'll discuss both in my follow-up on big data analysis.

Big data operates either by applying models to characterize a very large data set, or by "discovering" empirical patterns in the data. The example above is just such a discovery operation. The doctor enters data relevant to her patient and the system finds records with a (close to) identical pattern. It is then possible to determine things such as most effective treatment options from the set of records matching the current patient. Please note that this is not predictive, as mentioned above.

2. Big data is not machine learning: Machine learning is hard – The idea of it is relatively simple, but the design, development, and deployment of ML systems based on neural networks and other modules is complex and requires substantial computing resources as well as a good deal of specialized knowledge about statistical modeling and learning theory. This can be ameliorated by using any of the cloud-based ML engines that are available such as:

   a. (Google) TensorFlow – Currently available as open source software, TensorFlow is a data graph application where nodes are computational and edges are multidimensional data arrays (broadly tensors) that are computed on and communicated among nodes.

   b. Microsoft Azure – A cloud-based set of AI tools, which include data storage, ML tools, a "workbench," and integration with Microsoft SQL Server.

c. Amazon Web Services (AWS) – AWS offers a broad variety of ML and associated services, including both its own modeling and analytic tools and the ability to access external tools (like TensorFlow) in its cloud.

d. SAS System and many others.

Even with these systems, you have to decide what type of model (network structure and weighting strategy) to use and how to train the network. There are at least 30+ different types of networks currently in use, ranging from simple perceptrons (single layer neural networks) to deep convolutional and adversarial networks.* Each type of network represents a specific type of model tied to an execution strategy. Selection and training of these models require a good deal of expertise.

3. The details of ML are different, but many concepts and lessons learned are similar to those from earlier systems:

a. ML networks appear to be more effective using pre- and/or post-processing of data/results enhanced by various types of search (AlphaZero uses tree-based searches).

b. ML networks appear to be more effective using pre- and/or post-processing of data/results with rules or productions.

c. Representation matters – The way training data is structured can make training much more or much less effective.

d. Hyperlearning is a game changer – Hyperlearning, such as AlphaZero learning chess well enough in 4 hours, with no supervision or training set, to beat the strongest chess programs, will change the way we think about and use machine learning.

---

* https://en.wikipedia.org/wiki/Types_of_artificial_neural_networks/

Some Final (Not Really) Thoughts on AI

Will AI mean the end of humanity? – It's hard not to say something about this when such luminaries as (the late) Stephen Hawking, Elon Musk, Bill Gates, and others, including some prominent AI researchers, are very visibly of the opinion that AI in some form represents an existential threat to the human race. Most people of this opinion do not believe that a SkyNet*-like entity will actively wage war against humanity in order to eliminate us. No, it will be subtler than that. First will be the loss of jobs and the changes to social and cultural institutions that accompany this and other changes. Then, the subtle (and some not-so-subtle) biases in our intelligent systems will continue to cause the further evolution of sociocultural and economic systems. Next will come the consequences of the social and cultural changes as people's motivations and ambitions change, then the long decline …

I don't believe this. I don't believe that AI is inherently biased toward any specific set of outcomes, positive or negative, other than those that we initially program into it. AI is not, after all, some aggregated and integrated SkyNet-like entity, at least not yet. It's a set (and still a relatively small set) of programs and systems directed at various types of analysis and problem-solving. It is not developed in some pristine and culturally neutral background. Like all technology, it is developed in a social and cultural context that is partly the context of technology and technology development (male-dominated, quasi-egalitarian, etc.) and partly the national and regional contexts of the locations where it is developed.

What I do believe is that the potential development of a threat, perhaps not an existential one, but a serious one, is both possible and feasible. We must, therefore, first be aware of this

---

* *The Terminator* – 1984 movie directed by James Cameron, starring Arnold Schwarzenegger in which a national defense AI becomes "aware," decides that humans are a threat to its existence and wages war to eliminate them.

possibility, and second, actively work to develop this technology in such a way that we tend to minimize any such threat.
Is this easy? No. The culture of technology makes it harder (a
topic for another working paper). Do we fully understand what
it would mean to develop AI in this way? No. Some years ago
(in 1989), I had been invited to be on a panel (on the practice
of futurism) at a conference. One of the other panelists was Syd
Mead, the "visual futurist" who was responsible for the look of
the 1982 movie *Blade Runner.* At that point in his career, he
was working mostly for Japanese companies. He was not so
much designing near-future products but envisioning what their
medium- to longer-term products might look like and what the
environment they would be used in would look like. He and
I got into an argument after he stated that design and technology, in general, were socially neutral in a way that it had no
direct consequences. I stated, pretty strongly, that design and
technology were not only socially and culturally situated, but
also socially and culturally active in ways that technologists
had to take into account. The moderator finally stopped us, but
not before we had agitated the room. At that time, I estimated
that approximately 75% of the people present (almost all deep
techies) agreed with Syd Mead. I thought at the time (and still
do) that this was aspirational. Technologists would like to think
they have no social responsibilities, but they do.

Ethical development – There is a lot to this, but I'll be as
brief as possible (kinda) …

   i. Simplicity and understandability – This is really (for me)
      the core of everything. "It can scarcely be denied that
      the supreme goal of all theory is to make the irreducible
      basic elements as simple and as few as possible with-
      out having to surrender the adequate representation of
      a single datum of experience."* Simplicity, except in the

---

* A. Einstein, On the Method of Theoretical Physics, Herbert Spencer Lecture,
  Oxford University, June 10, 1933. Most probably the origin of the aphorism, also
  attributed to Einstein, "Everything should be as simple as possible, but no simpler."

most formal sense, such as in model theory,* is subjective. If something takes 47 closely spaced pages to explain, you might suspect that it could be simplified.

Very closely related to simplicity is understandability. One motivation for emphasizing simplicity is to improve the understandability of a model or analysis. This is one of the biggest criticisms of AI and machine-learning methods today – the fact that they are, for the most part, black boxes and the reasoning (in AI systems) and/or modeling and pattern recognition (in machine-learning systems) are so complex or random that they appear to be not understandable to mere humans. This does beg the question, though, that if mere humans can't understand the modeling or analytic process, how are they supposed to understand and believe the results produced by this process? Good question …

ii. Bias – There are two major dimensions to the problem of bias and the use of AI and machine learning. The first is data bias and the second is algorithm bias. Both of these problems are related to the fact that the collection and use of data, as well as the development and application of algorithms, are ultimately human activities that are embedded in social, organizational, and cultural contexts.

Data bias is probably pervasive and can greatly affect the operation and results of applying machine learning in particular to real-world problems. As detailed previously in this chapter, most machine-learning systems still are "trained" with sets of test or training data. The selection of these training sets determines how the system initially responds to the problem data that it is exposed to. Bias in training data usually takes the form of the data set only partially representing the universe of discourse of the problem. In healthcare, for instance, almost all large

---

* D.J. Hartzband, 1972, Eine Logik für das Ableiten der minimalen grundlegenden Annalmen für mehrfahe Modelle. Dissertation, University of Hamburg, Germany.

clinical data sets greatly under-represent minorities. This influences the machine-learning system such that the results it presents, the diagnosis of specific syndromes, for instance, are inaccurate with respect to the under-represented group(s). The footnote provides links to two recent articles on this topic.* Of course, this kind of bias is nothing new in healthcare and was an issue long before machine learning became the next shiny object in clinical care.[†] This is an extremely important issue that is only just beginning to be addressed.

The other side of the coin, algorithm bias, is just as important. This is also inevitable unless very deep steps are taken to prevent it. Algorithms are developed in social, cultural, and even organizational contexts, which ensures that the biases inherent in these institutions are represented in the machine-learning systems' underlying logic.[‡] This is quite difficult to detect and/or to correct. Knowing that it happens is an essential first step, but over time development processes will have to be adopted that help to ameliorate these biases. Independent review will need to be a core part of these processes.

iii. Don't be creepy – I recently attended a conference, in 2018, on the ethical use of "big data" in healthcare,[§] One of the keynote speakers was Farzad Mostashari, a former National Coordinator for Health Information Technology at the Department of Health and Human Services. Farzad is a favorite of mine – he can always be counted on to express important issues in his own style. He was speaking about his guidelines for doing research

---

* 2017, https://www.technologyreview.com/s/608986/forget-killer-robotsbias-is-the-real-ai-danger/, 2017, https://qz.com/1023448/if-youre-not-a-white-male-artificial-intelligences-use-in-healthcare-could-be-dangerous/
† https://www.ncbi.nlm.nih.gov/pmc/articles/PMC2594273/pdf/jnma00325-0024.pdf
‡ https://www.technologyreview.com/s/608986/forget-killer-robotsbias-is-the-real-ai-danger/
§ Health and ... Data Science and Public Action, NYU Langone School of Public Health, May 21, 2018.

with healthcare data. His primary admonition was "Don't be creepy." The work you are doing should not make people's skin crawl. The example he gave was that while he was at the Office of the National Coordinator for Healthcare Information Technology (ONC), a proposal was made to make people's healthcare records available to them only if they passed a credit check! This was truly creepy, unnecessary, and contrary to the whole spirit of providing care, especially in the safety net where I primarily worked. The use of AI and machine learning in any segment should not creep people out (leaving aside the situation where they are "creeped out" because they don't agree with the results). The sensibilities of the groups to whom the results refer must be taken into account in the design of AI and machine-learning studies and in the promulgation of their results.

Finally, the End (of AI and Machine Learning) ...

I have been working on the development of artificial intelligence, in one form or another, for about 40 years (seriously). If you had asked me in 1988, or even in 1998, whether some of the most interesting and important advances in computer science and real-world problem-solving would be coming from this area, I would have told you that the time was past for AI to have that kind of general influence – that there were areas where it would continue to be developed and deployed, but that it would not become a major force in everything from marketing strategy to chip development. I was wrong! I did not anticipate – and would not have anticipated – the importance and influence that machine learning would have. Over the past 5 years or so, I have been working with a good number of ML start-ups as well as some well-established companies developing ML, and I am struck by four things about these developments:

- The depth and breadth of the developments and the potential they have to improve our understanding in many, many fields of inquiry.
- The similarity of the foundations, as well as of many of the methods of design and reasoning of current ML systems, with earlier AI systems of various types (as detailed in this chapter).
- The enthusiasm of the people working on ML – This very much reminds me of the attitudes of people in the late 1970s and early 1980s, when we really thought that a general AI could be developed and applied to a wide range of problem-solving.
- The amount of resistance and pushback that accompanies technological developments that challenge the status quo both intellectually and culturally in established fields (e.g. healthcare).

All of this seems quite normal to me; if anything, the pace of development seems to have slowed, although this may be a symptom of so much of this work being done in corporate contexts, meaning that we do not have a total view of the progress that is being made. In any case, progress is being made, quickly, so that 5–8 years from now much of the application of this technology will seem "post-technical"* – that is, not visible as a separate technology, but simply part of how we do "stuff," whether that stuff is shopping or clinical research.

---

* It is not by chance that my consultancy is named PostTechnical Research – The idea is that a post-technical context is one where you do not notice your use of any specific technology ... you just do what you want/need to do and technology transparently supports you. I intend no value judgment about this (that's a topic for another white paper). It is just a fact that this will be the case for most people in the next 5–8 years – at least IMNSHO. Welcome to the "past-informed" future ...

Chapter 8

Evolution of Data and Analysis in Healthcare

Thinking about Data and Analytics

Healthcare Data in 2 Years … in 5 Years … in 20 Years

If we are to credibly project and understand the evolution of data and analytics in healthcare, we must first understand the evolution of the structure and use of information technology in healthcare. We can make projections for various timeframes based on current developments and trends, but we must also be able to look beyond current trends and try to determine what might be possible if we allow for organizational and cultural change. If we base our predictions only on current known trends, we'll limit our vision unnecessarily. Figure 8.1 maps out my projections for the coming 2, 5, and 20 years. Making projections for the coming 2 and 5 years is relatively straightforward, as current trends are the biggest influence in these timeframes. Attempting longer-term projections, such as for 20 years, is where the appreciation and integration of effort with a knowledge of organizational and cultural trends are essential. Once

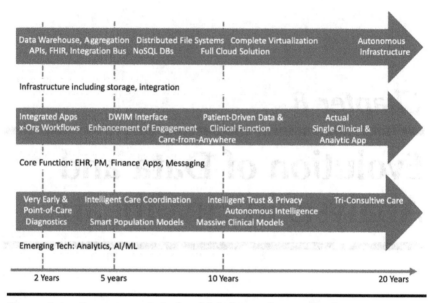

Figure 8.1   Future trends in health information technology.

these projections are explored, the evolution of the role of data and analytics over these timeframes can be addressed.

Figure 8.1 associates the relevant trends affecting each of the timeframes used for projection. The figure is organized along three dimensions: 1) infrastructure including storage and integration, etc.; 2) core function (apps) including electronic health record (EHR) systems, practice management, financial apps, and messaging, etc.; and 3) emerging technology, including analytics, AI/machine learning, etc.

Infrastructure

All three of these areas are strategic and changing quickly, but infrastructure is both the area least focused on and potentially the most strategic – as none of the other capabilities are possible without an evolved infrastructure. The endpoint of the description of the contemporary infrastructure for healthcare organizations was described in Chapter 6. This endpoint is made up of a parallel storage and application architecture.

One based on current relational technology with applications using data in the database's underlying core functions such as EHR or population health apps. This infrastructure will be sufficient but increasingly ineffective over the next 2–4 years. At 5 years and beyond, the volume and heterogeneity of the data, including many more types of sources, will require a move to the second architecture. This architecture is based on massively parallel distributed file systems and applications that are fully integrated with respect to both data and function. One of the forcing functions for this architecture is the integration of today's emerging technologies, such as machine learning and advanced analytics, into common use.

The evolution of the infrastructure dimension was explored in Chapter 6. The dimension in Figure 8.1 represents that evolution extended out 20 years. As already predicted, the current relational-based infrastructure and its individually and uniquely engineered applications may suffice for the next 2–4 years, but beyond that substantial changes will be required. The adoption of application programming interfaces (APIs) for easier (but not truly easy) interconnection between applications, as well as the use of standards such as FHIR for both data representation and the intercommunication of data, will extend our ability to use this architecture potentially for several more years. The cost of this extension, regardless of how comfortable it is to continue using current technologies, will be to push out the development and use of much more effective technologies and the new capabilities that they enable. One of the first areas for change to take place will necessarily be in data storage. The move away from relational databases to NoSQL systems has already happened for some applications designed and engineered in the last few years. The move allows almost unlimited amounts of data to be represented and stored, but NoSQL databases have many fewer tools and query facilities so that many functions, including things like transactional safety, are left as an exercise for the programmer. This is also true of many business intelligence and analytic capabilities. The move to fully distributed massively parallel file systems will complete the data storage evolution, at least for the next 5–7 years. Systems such as the Hadoop Distributed File System (HDFS), or systems based on HDFS, are engineered to be paired with some form of MapReduce (such as Yarn) for data analysis and can even support massively parallel SQL queries through modules such as Apache Hive. The move to these storage and analytics enabling systems in the next 5 years will allow the management and analysis of almost unlimited amounts of data. As we move past this timeframe, we'll see a move to the full virtualization of infrastructure so that dedicated systems supporting massive amounts of data can be encapsulated and moved from environment to environment with their operational and management functions intact. Finally, sometime between 10 and 20 years from now, we'll have the capability of what I'm calling "autonomous infrastructure." This is the ability of a system to flexibly provision an entire infrastructure based on the data in the system and its observation of what functions are necessary. There will obviously be other changes and capabilities developed in this dimension, but these are the primary ones that I see now.

Core Function

The next 5 years are going to see big changes in EHR and related application functions – they'll have to, as these applications have gotten too complex, too big, and too disconnected from the work and workflows of their users. In fact, recently, EHRs have been recognized as one of the primary causes of provider burnout.* The first set of changes I have characterized

---

* From the NEJM Catalyst event Physicians Leading | Leading Physicians at Intermountain Healthcare, July 12, 2017. Physicians are Facing a Crisis: EHR Burnout. *New England Journal of Medicine Catalyst*. https://catalyst. nejm.org/videos/physicians-facing-crisis-emr-burnout, accessed 2/20/2019; N.L. Downing, D.W. Bates, and C.A. Longhurst, 2018, Physician Burnout in the EHR Era: Are We Ignoring the Real Cause? *Annals of Internal Medicine*, 169(1): 50–51. https://annals.org/aim/article-abstract/2680726/ physician-burnout-electronic-health-record-era-we-ignoring-real-cause

as integrated applications. These are smaller, possibly simpler applications that work seamlessly together to present a complete picture of a patient's context, history, current status, etc. They would be modular and could be assembled as necessary given the role and need of the user. This would, of course, require a substantially more effective level of data access, interoperability, and data sharing than is currently possible, so we'd better get working on it. I really do not see any other way of achieving the necessary capabilities, especially as so many different types of data – everything from claims data to social determinants data to external (federal, state, etc.) data – will be needed. We simply cannot keep on enlarging current EHRs to encompass all of the data and functionality that will be required. It also goes without saying that although there may be billing applications of various types incorporated as modules, the design center for the suite of applications will not be billing, payment, and regulatory compliance. This emphasis is part of what got us here in the first place. (See Figure 8.2.)

It is also clear that another need driving greatly enhanced integration and interoperability will be cross-organizational workflows. We see these even now, as patients are moved from department to department or facility to facility, to receive care. Often the availability of a patient's records is difficult or not feasible as this journey progresses, even within the hospital or hospital system – even if they are using the same software. The continuity of care and the quality of a patient's care are greatly affected by these issues.

Current user interfaces for health information applications, regardless of platform, are awkward at best and serve as an impediment to care planning and treatment at worst. Some time ago, quite early in the development of AI-like capabilities, first for research applications and then commercial applications (the late 1960s to early 1970s), we developed an interface concept called DWIM, or Do What I Mean. The idea was to have the system or application anticipate the most probable

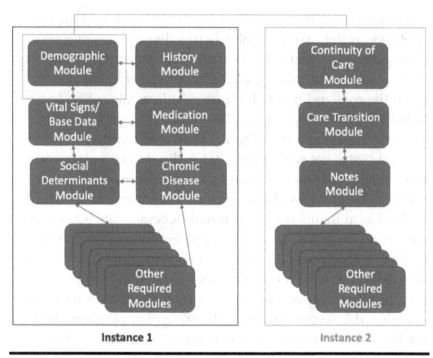

Figure 8.2   Modular EHR application.

next action by the user and to move the user to that part of
the interface that would enable the action – read my mind and
do what I mean. It was a great concept, but it was difficult
to develop, given the tools we had in the mid-1970s. It would
be much more feasible today. Probably the most advanced
instance was in BBN Lisp, written by Warren Teitelman (at
Xerox PARC).* Contemporary DWIM for healthcare would most
likely be applied to EHR interfaces. About 3 years ago, I did
an exercise at the HIMSS17 Conference (Health Information
Management System Society). I developed a use case where
a patient had multiple encounters for different problems. The
idea was to see how difficult it would be to record these
encounters in a variety of EHRs such that the comorbidities
involved would be evident from the patient's record. I worked

---

* https://en.wikipedia.org/wiki/DWIM

with people from six different EHRs and, in every case but one, the interface was too complicated (too many different forms, too many clicks, too many places to enter the same data) for a provider to enter the data to accurately reflect the patient's clinical situation. A DWIM-like interface that anticipated user action, moved the user to the correct place in the interface, and simplified the act of entering the patient's data would go a long way toward making EHR use more efficient and less frustrating.

The enhancement of engagement, of all types of users – providers, patients, caregivers, etc. – must also be greatly improved in order for our digital data ecosystem to function adequately in healthcare. Today's systems are primarily used based on the need for reimbursement and regulatory compliance. This is my observation over the past 15 years of working with people using these systems. Until these systems have the appeal of social media or gaming systems, we will not be able to really move forward in creating the digital healthcare ecosystem we want and need. In fact, these two areas might be good models for the development of increased engagement. Substantial work has been done on engagement factors in social media use,* and much of this might be relevant to health information technology (HIT) application engagement. Gaming has already been used as a model.[†]

Somewhere in the 5–7 year timeframe, I have an element: "care-from-anywhere." This represents the evolution of the modular suite of functions discussed above to be able to run on "any" device – from mobile devices of various types to large-scale distributed infrastructure that will be used for

---

* M. Dodard, 2017, The Psychology Behind Social Media Engagement, https://www.socialmediatoday.com/social-business/psychology-behind-social-media-engagement, accessed February 20, 2019.
† D. Gibbs, B. Hewitt, and A. Mcleod, 2016, The Gamification of Electronic Health Records: A Systematic Literature Review. *Educational Perspectives in Health Informatics Information Management*, AHIMA. https://eduperspectives.ahima.org/the-gamification-of-electronic-health-records-a-systematic-literature-review/, accessed February 20, 2019.

storage and analysis of massive amounts of data, and every type of system in between. Modules may have different instances, with the same functions, optimized for different operating environments, but all modules will be integrated with respect to functionality and interoperable with respect to data (see the section on "Some Thoughts on Integration" in Chapter 6).

We have been working toward "patient-centered care" for some time now. I have always taken this to mean focusing on the patient, as opposed to the payer, the hospital/clinic, or even the provider, as the core of healthcare delivery. I have described (on my blog) a different patient focus that I am calling patient-driven data and clinical function in my predictions. In this model of care, the patient is not only the center of care, but is also the center of those elements that contribute to care. This includes data. Patients, at this time, will not only have access to their entire medical record(s), but will also have access to summary, analytic, and clinical assessment tools that will enable them to contribute to their healthcare data as well as get a set of analyses relevant to their medical and societal context. They will also be able to see a set of recommendations for clinical function/intervention and have tools to assess them and discuss them with their provider(s). The idea here is not to replace providers with care that the patient directs, but to give the patient enough access and additional information to be able to participate in care planning and medical decision-making. We say this is possible today, but patients have far too little data, information, analysis, and context to actually participate, except at the levels of likes and dislikes, in their care planning and execution.

Finally, with respect to core function, I specify an "actual single clinical and analytic application." This is an application that would be used by both the provider, including the care team, and the patient, and would provide each with the breadth of data (medical facts related to a specific patient, or in some cases population), analysis, and recommendation necessary to carry out the best possible (at the time) patient care. Such an application would be the endpoint of the 20-year evolution of the provision of core function.

Emerging Technology

The emerging technology dimension includes analytics, AI/ machine learning, advanced integration and interoperability function, even more massive data models, human–machine collaboration, and other capabilities. The first milestone, one that is already in the early stages of development and use, is point-of-care diagnostics, which enable the very early detection of health problems. Many large and small enterprises are working on or supplying these types of systems, ranging from Kaiser Permanente, to IBM Watson Healthcare, to Google Brian and Deep Mind, to much smaller enterprises that specialize in a specific area of diagnosis. These systems work by running in the background as a provider enters data at the patient's point-of-care. The system is most often a deep learning model (multi-layer neural network representing a specific type of statistical and/or mathematical model, such as classification or regression) with an EHR-like user interface that can analyze a massive data store of healthcare data. As more data is entered, it informs the provider that it may have discovered some specific number of cases that match the parameters being entered for this particular patient. Let's say the system informs the provider that it has located 3451 cases matching the current case. That is an empirical fact – the system has located 3451 cases – not a statistical one. The data set needs to be sufficiently large – for example, Kaiser Permanente is said to have in the range of 40 petabytes (PBs) of patient data (9.5 million records over 15 years). The system will extract the most common outcomes and the associated treatment plans, and it will also make recommendations for the best treatment plan. Part of the system's response may be to inform the provider that the patient should be checked for specific problems that have not been part of their history – such as an incipient cancer of some type. Many of the organizations that are already using such systems have had to develop guidelines for usage. The provider has the responsibility for treating the patient and so has the final responsibility for deciding upon that treatment. They can take the machine input into account in whole, in part, or not at all (although increasingly they will have to justify their decisions in this matter). Ten years from now, "I'm the doctor" may not be an adequate rationale for ignoring machine input. These systems will increasingly work with the provider, eventually in all areas of medicine (clinical, research, etc.). I'll discuss this collaboration in more detail as the endpoint of this dimension.

Two of the biggest impediments to providing optimal care today are 1) maintaining the continuity of care and 2) performing appropriate care transitions. These are related, complex operations involving data sharing and communications across a care team that may span organizations and facilities, and may require shared decision-making that includes the patient and/or caregiver. The coordination of workflows and the required data for these operations are currently done by a combination of EHR use and access, messaging among team members, e-mail (often unsecured), the transfer of notes and clinical data, the use of separate, non-EHR-based systems for the coordination of financial and consent processes, and sometimes just calling the mobile phones of team members to ensure that a critical step is or will be performed. Such activity depends on mechanisms such as checklists, shared notes and files describing workflows, collaboration software not related to the EHR system, and many other "devices." It is clear that there is a good deal of room for misunderstanding, delay, and error in this overall process, any of which can affect the health of the patient and the ultimate outcome of their care.

The use of an enhanced or intelligent workflow system would certainly facilitate a care team's ability to provide timely and accurate care. This would greatly improve the patient's health at the time as well as the overall outcome. Such systems could be integrated with the EHR system so that the team members' workflows would not be interrupted by the use of a separate system. Ideally, in the next 3–5 years, these intelligent care modules would become a module in the evolved healthcare information system, as described in the previous section. It is possible that other intelligent care modules would be developed as needed, such as treatment modules that identified comorbidities or suites of related conditions that could have a combined treatment plan developed for the patient. The identification of comorbidities from EHR data is often problematic, because many records do not show multiple diagnoses, even if there are clear relations between the treated problems. There are many reasons for this, as discussed in Hartzband and Jacobs.*

So much has been written and predicted regarding AI/ machine learning in healthcare that it seems redundant to say much about it in terms of the future state of health information technology. Suffice to say that, at this time (winter 2019), we are already seeing this technology being productively used, especially in diagnosis. Several years ago, the famous (or infamous depending on where your product/technology falls on it) hype cycle curve positioned machine learning at the highest point of the Peak of Exaggerated Expectations.† Several recent updates have moved it through the Trough of Disillusionment out to the Path of Enlightenment. (See Figure 8.3.) This indicates that opinion now believes that AI/ML is being used, at least by some advanced organizations, productively and that this will increasingly become the case. I have predicted the relatively common use of "autonomous intelligence" in a 5–8-year timeframe. By this, I mean that the integrated healthcare information systems I have been writing about will have the

---

* D.J. Hartzband and F. Jacobs, 2016, Deployment of Analytics into the Healthcare Safety Net: Lessons Learned. *Online Journal of Public Health Information.*
† Gartner, 2016, Healthcare Hype Cycle. https://dminc.com/blog/ artificial-intelligence-euphoria-healthcare-life-sciences/

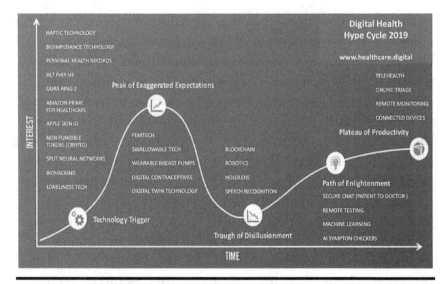

Figure 8.3   2019 Digital health hype cycle.*

capability to provide diagnosis, treatment planning, feedback on outcomes, and operational suggestions – as well as make suggestions for improved clinical workflows and non-clinical processes in real time as work is being done. The provider or administrator will not have to explicitly ask for this advice, it will be available as a sidebar to their work. There are several design concepts that are important here – actually, that are important for AI/ML today as well. The first is explanation: ML systems today mainly function as black boxes. How the layers of neural nets provide a set of results can be inferred but not exactly explained (for the most part). My experience in developing AI-based systems – and, actually, mathematical model-based systems – is that people are generally skeptical of black boxes. They are not willing to accept results from a system unless some form of understandable explanation for how the results were arrived is available. The explanation does not have to be comprehensive, but it does need to be understandable at a high level.

* https://www.healthcare.digital/single-post/2019/01/12/
  The-Digital-Health-Hype-Cycle-2019

The second concept is that such "advice," whether it's from an ML system, or the EHR, or a colleague, needs to be provided in a way that does not disrupt the workflow of the user – a provider, an administrator, or other staff. There are several ways of doing this. Perhaps the best way is to incorporate the advice stream directly into the interface (user experience) of the application providing the workflow. That way the user, let's say a provider, doesn't have to leave their primary application in order to receive and act upon the advice (in much the same way as accessing the EHR system). If this type of intimate integration is not technically feasible, the advice stream can be provided side-by-side with the primary application, or as a sidebar to it, providing minimal disruption, as the user can simply look at the material in the sidebar.

The final concept for this prediction is that of advice. There are many predictive systems under development, and some even in use in healthcare today. They tend to be more accepted by users* if they provide advice rather than proscriptive instructions. Users, especially clinicians, want to make their own mind up about diagnosis, treatment planning, etc. They do not want to be "told" by a system what the proper course of action is, even if they agree. If the system is couched as an advisor, that is much more acceptable than if it is couched as the authority.

We've already looked at the exponential increase in the healthcare data that will be available for utilization in treatment planning and execution in the next 3, 5, and 8 years. The amount of healthcare data appears to be doubling every 2 years (see Chapter 4, the section on "Data in Context,"). If most healthcare organizations will have around 3–5 terabytes (TBs) of data in 5 years' time, with many having up to 100 TBs, and the biggest organizations having more than 1 PB, then one of the most important design considerations for health information systems will be how to manage and

---

* Personal observation.

analyze this amount of data. Using these large amounts of data to develop clinical, and especially population, models is quite different from our current process. As already stated, using this amount of data may actually provide empirical rather than statistical models (of course all aggregated models are ultimately statistical). In this context, this means that there is enough data for the model to be based on actual data rather than sampled and/or statistically predicted data. This gives the model a different posture in terms of accuracy and believability. In such models, statistical error can be vanishingly small.* How such models are expressed or interpreted is still a work in progress.

Two areas that have received a lot of attention since the advent of electronic health records are trust and privacy. These areas are inseparable from security and have become increasingly important as patients and the people around them take more and more responsibility for their care. The importance of privacy is immediately obviously. Patient's healthcare is specific to them and to them only. People who are not involved directly in their care, or in managing or administering to those involved, should not be able to have access to an individual's data – to *my* data. If data cannot be kept private, then the whole system starts to break down. If data cannot be kept private, the trust between the patient, their family, caregivers, etc., and the patient's medical providers breaks down. This applies to both the medical and non-medical institutions involved in their care.

More and more, however, the impetus to improve care and patient outcomes means that data of all kinds must be aggregated and shared in order to provide the best treatment and "care-from-anywhere" that is possible. Several years ago, I was talking with John Mattison, MD, who was then chief medical information officer (CMIO) for Kaiser Permanente (Northern

---

* Statistical standard error in a universe with millions of samples can be as low as a millionth of the mean, or lower.

California). We were speaking about Health Information Exchanges (HIEs) and some of the issues that were acting as impediments to the adoption of this data-sharing model. He remarked to me that "Data flows at the speed of trust." This is quite true – there were, and still are, technological issues with the kind of data sharing that HIEs provide, but the primary issues were and continue to be organizational and cultural ones. Primary among these is the issue of trust. I don't remember how many times I've had otherwise quite reasonable providers or healthcare administrators tell me, "These are my patients. Why should I share their data?" This is often true even when they understand that the data is being shared so that another provider, either geographically or organizationally separated from them, is actually treating the patient. In the past 10 years or so, a model of trust has been developed to ameliorate this issue.* This model is based on a trust framework composed of:

a. *Trust model* – The trust model is at the core of the framework. It describes the elements of a trusted system and explains their relationships and how the elements generate and maintain trust among the members of the trust community.

b. *General policy taxonomy* – The general policy taxonomy provides the policy context for the trust model. It defines the privacy risks and the mechanisms to ameliorate them at the general level. This taxonomy is relevant to information sharing in general, not just for healthcare. Specializations of the taxonomy can be made for specific verticals such as healthcare.

---

* I was the principal investigator on a National Institute for Standards and Technology (NIST) grant that addressed this topic as part of a project on internet-based identity verification, and I worked extensively on this issue at the time: Identity Ecosystem for Patient-Centered Co-ordination of Care Project (PCC), NIST, National Strategy for Trusted Identities in Cyberspace (NSTIC), 70NANB12D296. September 2012–September 2014.

    c. *Target segment* – This refers to the specific policies associated with the exchange that the trust model represents; for example, it could be exchanged though through the direct protocol between general providers at a community clinic and cardiac specialists at a regional hospital, or any number of other specific exchanges.

    d. *Enforced policies* – The set of top-down policies, primarily derived from federal legislation or federal and state regulations and guidelines that define the large-scale policy requirements for privacy, security, information usage, etc., that must be met by the system, and the set of bottom-up policies primarily derived from the information and operational policies of the specific exchange represented.

Trust frameworks are used by HIEs, Accountable Care Organizations (ACOs), and other organizations doing exchange of healthcare information in order to increase confidence that identity, privacy, and security measures are in place, and being monitored and enforced as part of the exchange process. The idea here would be to make the policies and processes that make up the trust framework intelligent so that much of the work of establishing and maintaining the exchange is done automatically. This would greatly improve both the probability that data exchange would take place and that it would be correct and protected, which, in turn, would help to improve patient care and outcomes.

    The endpoint of these emerging technologies is what I am calling "tri-consultive care." This is the full collaboration of a) the provider and/or care team; b) the patient, including caregivers, family members, and other involved people; and c) the cognitive system of some type. It concerns all aspects of preventative care, diagnosis, care planning, and necessary care transitions. In order to do this, cognitive systems in healthcare will have had to evolve from the first examples we have today – the point-of-care diagnosis systems already discussed – to systems that are really capable of an interactive discourse with providers and patients. This is much more than a natural language interface, although that will be essential. It also includes:

- A deep and broad data set that is drawn from highly diverse sources
- The ability to infer context from the data so that it can be interpreted as information
- The ability to develop appropriate analytic models and to interpret the results of those models
- The ability to identify and interpret conventional and unconventional patterns in the data/information set
- The ability to convey context and the results of model development and pattern matching in productive ways that increase the understanding of a patient's situation and potential outcomes
- The ability to interact with other involved parties as a collaborative partner

A system that could operate like this could and would be thought of as a partner in the patient's care and could greatly enhance the understanding, by all parties, of a patient's situation as well as the patient's outcomes. Of course, as with any "technological" advance, the real issues are in the organizational and cultural aspects of the development and adoption of new systems, so two things will be especially important for this development to take hold.

1. The system will need to be collegial, that is, not prescriptive or overbearing. The system attitude will need to truly be consultive and collaborative.
2. The system will need to provide backup and explanation for its recommendations. This is, in fact, true for any intelligent healthcare system.

The endpoint of these predictions, coming into existence 15–20 years from now, will be a healthcare information system that has a self-configuring, just-in-time infrastructure that is capable of managing and providing huge amounts of data to be used in analysis with a useful and usable interface that does not require a deep understanding of anything other than clinical data. Users will interact through an advanced and predictive interface with a single integrated application that is modular and provides both clinical and analytic capability. This application will integrate diagnostics, treatment, and population models, and be able to fully use clinical data, claims data, social determinants data, and, in fact, any relevant data, to present a consultive and collaborative "face" to all those involved in a patient's care. I have only discussed the clinical side of this HIT evolution with these predictions, but there is an administrative side to these systems that will provide parallel capabilities (eventually consultive and collaborative capabilities) to non-clinical people working in healthcare as well.

The Evolution of the Role of Data and Analytics

We are deeply involved in a transformation of healthcare and healthcare information technology. I have outlined some of the changes I believe will need to take place over the medium term (the next 5–20 years). These changes are influenced by the changes that are occurring in our understanding and use of both data and analytics. In order to describe the changes in data and analytics, we need to first describe some of the forces that are causing these changes. Most of these have been covered in some way up until now in this text, but a summary would be good here. Figure 8.4 shows some of the scope of the data that will be required and some of the forcing functions that are influencing the evolution of data and analytics. I have already discussed a) the implications of the massive amounts of data that are becoming available in terms of emerging technologies (data management infrastructure, machine learning and analytics, etc.); b) related to this, the

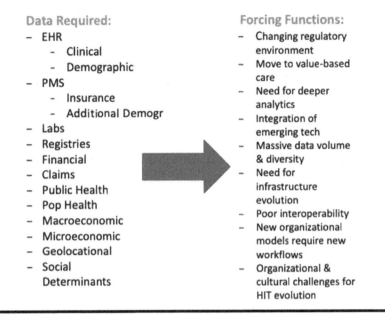

Data Required:
- EHR
  - Clinical
  - Demographic
- PMS
  - Insurance
  - Additional Demogr
- Labs
- Registries
- Financial
- Claims
- Public Health
- Pop Health
- Macroeconomic
- Microeconomic
- Geolocational
- Social Determinants

Forcing Functions:
- Changing regulatory environment
- Move to value-based care
- Need for deeper analytics
- Integration of emerging tech
- Massive data volume & diversity
- Need for infrastructure evolution
- Poor interoperability
- New organizational models require new workflows
- Organizational & cultural challenges for HIT evolution

Figure 8.4   Forcing functions for data evolution.

integration of emerging technologies into the HIT architecture and usage; and c) the poor state of interoperability in this environment. I'll, therefore, focus on the implications of the move to value-based care, which actually touches almost all of these areas.

The first thing we need to do is define value-based care.* An article in *The New England Journal of Medicine* defined value-based care as follows:

> Value-based healthcare is a healthcare delivery model in which providers, including hospitals and physicians, are paid based on patient health outcomes. Under value-based care agreements, providers are rewarded for helping patients improve their health, reduce the effects and incidence of chronic disease, and live healthier lives in an evidence-based way.

---

* https://catalyst.nejm.org/what-is-value-based-healthcare/

Value-based care differs from a fee-for-service or capitated approach, in which providers are paid based on the amount of healthcare services they deliver. The "value" in value-based healthcare is derived from measuring health outcomes against the cost of delivering the outcomes.

What does this mean in terms of care delivery? Value-based care emphasizes:

- Team-based care
- Population health analysis and intervention
- Cost-efficient care, where value is measured by lowering the cost of positive outcomes

The implication for data and analysis is that they have to be focused on these dimensions, that is:

- Team-based approaches for individual care as well as effective care continuity and transition
  - New diagnosis and treatment models and processes
  - Data sharing to facilitate these goals
  - New organizational and functional models to facilitate these goals (ACOs, HIEs, e-referral (Direct))
  - New workflow models to facilitate these goals
- Population data including social determinants of health
  - New approaches to data analysis, including:
    - Management of heterogeneous data
    - Visualization of population characteristics
    - Development of predictive models for population health status
  - New approaches to evidence (data)-based interventions
- Assembly and management of heterogeneous data sets to facilitate cost analysis (including claims and cost accounting data)
  - New models for the analysis of cost
  - New models for relating cost to treatment outcomes

The two most important changes here are:

1. The technical and organizational changes needed to calculate value, that is the cost of providing healthcare outcomes
2. The development of new data and analytic models to facilitate this calculation

What comes after value-based care? I recently attended the HIMSS19 Conference.* I spoke with quite a number of people there about their views on value-based care, its feasibility, what progress had been made, etc. I got, as you might imagine, a wide range of answers – everything from "it's here, we're reaping the benefits now" (admittedly not so many of these) to "it has already failed, let's admit it and move on" (more than I thought I'd get). The consensus was, as consensuses generally are, somewhere in the middle. I was surprised, however, by the larger-than-I-thought number of people who thought that value-based care as an idea was a terrific idea but not practical given the structure of the current system. Many of these people suggested that if cost reduction was the goal, then the only way to achieve it would be through restrictive price controls set by government regulation. That didn't seem to be feasible politically, regardless of party or ideology, so many people felt that we would have to muddle through with various types of government interventions that would be less effective than we would like.

I actually do not believe that this is the inevitable outcome. I do not know if we can make the current version of value-based care work to lower cost and improve both patient outcomes and population health, but I do know that none of these changes I have predicted and described here will work unless patients are much more involved in making decisions about their health.

---

* Health Information Management Systems Society Conference, February 10–15, 2019, Orlando, FL.

In each of my predictive dimensions, I emphasized user and/or patient involvement. In the infrastructure dimension, I described the concept of autonomous infrastructure, that is, taking the user out of the design and provisioning of the HIT infrastructure. This may seem counterintuitive, but the development will take this responsibility out of the hands of the IT staff and free them up for more user-facing (administrator, provider, and patient) interactions.

In the core function dimension, I described a patient-driven data and clinical function capability. In this element, the patient is not only the center of care but also the center of all those elements that relate to providing care, including data. This means that the data is, at least initially, organized around the patient as opposed to any other dimension it could be organized around. This, in turn, influences all other efforts on behalf of the patient.

Finally, in the emerging technology dimension, I described the "tri-consultive care" element, where the intelligent system, the provider (care team), and the patient collaborate seamlessly and equally in care planning and execution. It has long been a tenet of healthcare economics that the involvement of the patient and the patient's support group, at all levels of clinical decision-making, will, in the vast majority cases, lower costs and improve outcomes. This, more than anything, may be the key to actual, as opposed to regulatory, mandated, value-based care.

Chapter 9

Summary

I'm starting my summary with a word and phrase frequency analysis of this text. The reason for this is that an examination of the most frequently used words and phrases will provide a summary of the themes and dimensions that are important to the topics of data and data use in healthcare, and this set of themes and dimensions can be used to structure this review and summary of the book. Figure 9.1 and Figure 9.2 present the results of this analysis, first, as a bar chart of the 12 most frequently used words and, second, the 12 most frequently used phrases in this text.

Word and Phrase Frequency Analysis – This Text*

If we look at the 12 most frequently used words in the text they are:

1. Data (882 occurrences)
2. Health, healthcare, and variations (183)

---

* http://www.writewords.org.uk/word_count.asp

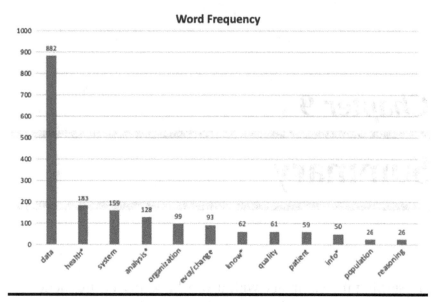

Figure 9.1   Word frequency analysis of this text.

3. System (159)
4. Analysis (128)
5. Organization (99)
6. Know, knowledge and variations (62)
7. Quality (61)
8. Patient (59)
9. Information and variations (50)
10. Population (26)
11. Reasoning (26)

If we look at a similar list for the frequency of word phrases in this text, it would be:

1. Data quality (35)
2. Data governance (31)
3. Machine learning (31)
4. Healthcare organization (30)
5. Healthcare information/data (25)

Phrase Frequency

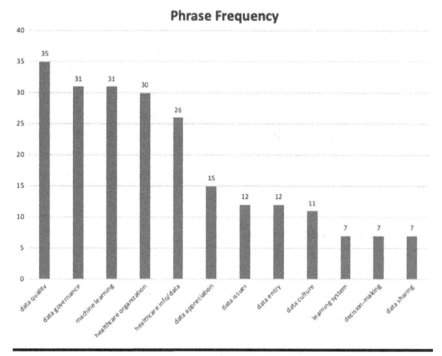

Figure 9.2   Phrase frequency – this text.

6. Data appreciation (15)
7. Data issues (12)
8. Data entry (12)
9. Data culture (11)
10. Learning system (7)
11. Decision-making (7)
12. Data sharing (7)

If we look at the word frequencies, the word data overwhelms all other occurrences. This should not be surprising, as this is a book about data, what it is, and how it is used in healthcare. Information also occurs in this list, so that data and information are, of course, a major theme. The second cluster is knowledge, knowing, and the associated words, analysis, and reasoning, which constitute a second major theme. Patients and populations are a third theme, and quality is a fourth.

If we look at the phrase frequencies, 7 of the 12 most frequent phrases have to do with data. These phrases fill out the nuances of the data theme identified from word frequencies. A secondary aspect of this theme is healthcare information. Machine learning and learning systems are two important phrases on the list, and these indicate a theme of human and non-human learning. The final theme indicated in the frequency analysis of phrases is decision-making. To summarize, these analyses identify the following themes from the frequency analysis of words and phrases in this text:

- ■ **Data and information**
    - – Data culture, appreciation, and sharing
    - – Data quality
- ■ **Knowledge, analysis, and reasoning**
    - – Human and non-human learning
    - – Decision-making
- ■ **Patients and populations**
    - – Healthcare data

Figure 9.3 proposes a relationship graph between these themes.

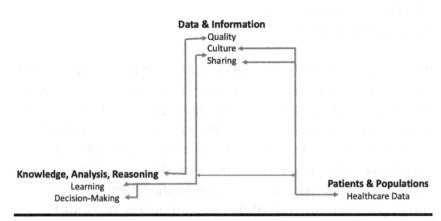

Figure 9.3   Major themes from text analysis.

Data and Information

In Chapter 2, we defined data as "facts derived from measurement or analysis that can be useful, irrelevant, or redundant and that generally must be processed in some way to be interpretable." We know that "facts are statements about the world," and we still know facts directly from their statement; and, at least in science and medicine, we base our belief in these facts on our ability to verify them. We establish facts either by direct measurement or by the analysis of direct measurement (derived facts).

Healthcare data, then, is taken from the verifiable facts relating to an individual's or group's health. When your doctor reports on your blood pressure, your random plasma glucose, or on an image of an ambiguous skin blemish, those facts are verifiable in a number of ways including:

- Repeated measurement at the time
- Repeated measurement over time
- Comparison with expected norms

Any significant changes in these measurements is a discrepancy in verifiability and should be investigated further. These three verification strategies are directly related not only to our belief in individual facts but also to the closely related concept of data quality. Any anomaly in verification can imply a data quality issue that should be investigated. As we saw, the complex practice of data governance has been developed to address the causes of these anomalies, but the practice of governance is not always feasible. Very large amounts of data may make it difficult or close to impossible to "govern" the data. In addition, data entry and processing practices, whether they are legacy practices or newly adopted, can also make conventional governance processes impractical. In these cases, actually in all current cases, it may be more practical and effective to use what I've described as a pragmatic comparative or "backcasting" method for examining data issues (Level-Up) that has proved effective in several recent studies and projects carried out by the author (see Chapter 4, Data Issues, section on "Data Issues and What Can Be Done about Them").

Another aspect of ensuring data quality, and an especially important aspect of data governance, is data culture. Culture can be defined as the social behavior and norms of a human society or group.* Data culture, by extension, is the social behavior and norms of a group as related to data. Two aspects of this culture were explored (Chapter 3):

- Data appreciation
- Data awareness

Knowledge, Analysis, and Reasoning

Unfinished.

Patients and Populations

Unfinished.

---

* https://en.wikipedia.org/wiki/Culture

Index

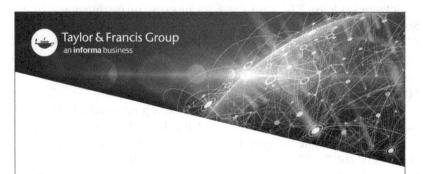